A BASIC CHURCH DICTIONARY

Tony Meakin was a parish priest for almost thirty-five years. He spent his last five years of active ministry as the Bishop of Durham's Senior Chaplain. Now retired, he is an Honorary Canon Emeritus of Durham Cathedral and lives in Burnopfield, near Newcastle upon Tyne.

From reviews of the earlier editions:

'Provides concise and useful summaries of biblical and ecclesiastical terms'
— *Church Times*

'A valuable reference tool for almost anyone with an interest in the Church and Christianity'
— *Northern Echo*

'An absolute necessity for every PCC Secretary, Incumbent and Church member'
— *The Sign*

'An excellent little book for reference in the class or school library'
— *Welsh RE News*

A Basic Church Dictionary

Revised and Expanded Edition

Compiled by

TONY MEAKIN

CANTERBURY
PRESS
Norwich

First edition 1990; reprinted with amendments 1992;
Revised, enlarged and illustrated edition published 1995.
Revised third edition published in 1999
Revised fourth edition (to include Common Worship references)
Published in 2001
by The Canterbury Press Norwich
(a division of SCM-Canterbury Press Ltd, a subsidiary of
Hymns Ancient & Modern Ltd, a registered charity)
St Mary's Works, St Mary's Plain,
Norwich, Norfolk, NR3 3BH

British Library Cataloguing in Publication Data

A catalogue record for this book is available
from the British Library

ISBN 1–85311–420–0

*Typeset by Rowland Phototypesetting Ltd,
Bury St Edmunds, Suffolk
and printed in Great Britain by
St Edmundsbury Press Ltd, Bury St Edmunds, Suffolk*

Contents

Acknowledgements

The author is grateful to the following for permission to reproduce extracts from: The *Book of Common Prayer* 1662, the rights of which are vested in the Crown in the United Kingdom, Eyre & Spottiswoode (Publishers) Ltd; *Common Worship*, *The Canons of the Church of England*, *The Christian Year: Calendar, Lectionary and Collects*, copyright the Archbishops' Council of the Church of England; also the following for allowing use of material from: *Concise Oxford Dictionary* and *Oxford Dictionary of the Christian Church*, Oxford University Press, *Dictionary of Christian Theology*, S.C.M. Press Ltd. *New Jerusalem Bible* (Old and New Testaments), Darton, Longman and Todd Ltd.; *Peak's Commentary on the Bible*, Thomas Nelson and Sons Ltd.

The Author is also grateful to the following for illustrations: B.T. Batsford Ltd, pp 70–75, from *Parish Church Architecture*; SPCK, London, 1964, pp 137, 138, used by permission of the publishers from *Saints, Signs and Symbols*, W. Ellwood Post: © 1962, 1974 by Morehouse-Barlow Co; p. 72, by the late Arnold Mitchell, FRIBA, from *A Guide to English Gothic Architecture*, Samuel Gardener, Cambridge University Press, 1922; also to Danielle Paul for illustrations on pp. 84 and 86; and to Clive Edwards for the illustrations on pp. 66–68, 76, 78, 90, 106–8.

Foreword – The Rt Revd Lord Habgood, Archbishop of York 1983–95

Every activity these days develops its own specialist jargon and the Church, which has been at it for longer than most, is no exception. Some words are highly technical, and almost anybody might be forgiven for rubbing their eyes a little if they read, for example, that the Dean of the Arches had ordered the removal of a lozenge from the narthex.

Other words are part of our common vocabulary, but are frequently misunderstood. And there is, unfortunately, a growing number of people for whom familiar words often used in church, or about churches, are completely mystifying.

This book will help all those who feel baffled or bewildered, or who just enjoy good, clear definitions of familiar things. It is well arranged and can be studied both alphabetically and also in terms of broad subjects. This means that a reader in need of enlightenment, say, on clerical wear, or on Church government, can read a grouped series of definitions without having to search for scattered separate entries.

I can warmly commend it.

✠ John Habgood

Preface

After more than forty years in the Anglican ministry and a wide experience of teaching, and preaching, it has become evident to me how specialised is the vocabulary we use in every corner of the Church's life. There are the 'jargon' words of theology and the words connected with the organisation and government of the Church, the Ministry, Church architecture and Church contents, Church music, the Church's Year, Church services, creeds and books. At the same time, many people find it difficult to understand just how the Church of England works, not only in its structure but also in its worship. This book tries to help with both problems. It is neither original, nor does it attempt to go into great detail. It simply seeks to explain – and hopefully to enthuse its readers to look further. We take so many 'Church' words for granted – there are so many 'Church' matters and words which are not understood. This book will, I hope, serve to enlarge people's grasp of their meanings and so help them to become better informed members of the Church of England.

The use of asterisks* throughout the text indicates that a word so marked is defined elsewhere, and can be found by consulting the Dictionary section. If a word occurs more than once within a particular definition, it is only asterisked the first time.

I would like to express my thanks to Samuel Cutt, former Canon and Treasurer of Wells, for his invaluable comments and corrections, to Jeremy Haselock, Canon Precentor of Norwich, for his greatly appreciated help with the transition to *Common Worship*, to Christine Smith and Clive Edwards of The Canterbury Press Norwich, Andrew Roberts of the General Synod Office, and Irene Ridley, Anne Lindsley and Anne Williams for their indispensable help and advice, but most of all to Ann, David, Paul and Helen, without whose encouragement and understanding this book would never have been written.

TONY MEAKIN

Part One: A Basic Church Dictionary

A Basic Church Dictionary

Abacus 77

Abba (see **Aramaic**) The Aramaic word for 'Father'. Aramaic was the popular language of Israel in our Lord's time, and almost certainly the language he used. '*Abba*' is a term of endearment akin to the English 'Daddy' (see Mark 14.36, Romans 8.15, Galatians 4.6).

Abbey 77

Abbot 49

Ablutions 105

Absolution 30, 48, 49, 105, 118

Abutment 77

Acclamation (Latin – *clamare* – to shout) To shout in a person's honour e.g. the acclamations in C.W.* Holy Communion* service, Order One – 'Christ* has died, Christ is risen, Christ will come again', and in the Marriage* Service –
'Priest*: Blessed are you, Heavenly Father:
All: You give joy to bridegroom and bride etc.'

Acolyte 105

Acts 130

Acts, manual 112

A.D. = *Anno Domini* (Latin) In the year of our Lord. The current system of dating, using the supposed year of our Lord's birth as the dividing point between B.C. (Before Christ) and A.D. was devised by Dionysius Exiguus who died c. A.D. 550. To make grammatical sense, the letters A.D. should always come before the number of the year. The letters B.C. should follow the number. It is thought that the actual year of our Lord's birth fell somewhere between 7 B.C. and 4 B.C.

Adonai (Hebrew – majesty) A name for God used frequently in the Old Testament* (see Yahweh).

Advent 97

Advent, Sundays before 102

Advent, Sundays of 98

Advocate (Latin – *advocare* – to call) One who pleads for another. A title of the Holy Spirit* used by our Lord in St John's Gospel*, and of our Lord himself in the 1st Letter of John*. They are foremost in pleading on our behalf that the Father's mercy may be shown to us. The Greek word used in this sense of the Holy Spirit is '*parakletos*' – '*para*' beside, '*kaleo*' – call (Paraclete*).

Advowson 58

Affinity, Degrees of (Latin – *affinis* – neighbouring, connected with) Affinity is a relationship created by a valid marriage*. By virtue of this relationship, restrictions on the possibility of marriages between certain blood relations of the couple forming the original relationship are imposed. These restrictions are listed in a 'Table of Kindred and Affinity' and are known as the prohibited degrees.

Affusion (Latin – *fundere* – to pour) The method of baptism* now usually practised in the Western Church* whereby water* is poured over the head of the candidate.

After Trinity, Sundays 102

Agape 21, 105

Agnus Dei 95

Aisle 77

Alb 65, 67, 68

Alleluia (Hebrew – 'praise *ye Yah*' (God)) A shout of praise used in both the Old and New Testaments* and frequently used in Christian worship* and hymns*.

All Hallows 16

Alms 106

Alpha and Omega 87, 137

Altar 77, 78, 79, 106

Altar book 106

Altar cloth 106

Altar, high 85

Altar, nave 87

Altar of repose 77

Altar rails 77, 78

Ambo 77, 110

Ambulatory 77

A.M.D.G. 137

Amen (Hebrew) A word meaning 'truly' or 'so be it'. It is used by both Jews and Christians to signify personal agreement and identification with the thoughts expressed in prayers*, hymns* and creeds*.

Amice 65, 67

Amos, Book of the Prophet 128

Anamnesis 106

Anaphora 106

Anastasis (Greek – resurrection) From the first, the word used of the resurrection both of Christ* and of the human race in general.

Anathema (Greek, later meaning, accursed thing) In former days, the curse of the Church* pronounced upon a person or a doctrine*.

Ancient of Days Or 'one aged in days'. A title of Yahweh* found in the Book of Daniel* which conveys no idea of eternity, but simply of longevity.

Angel (Greek – *aggelos* – messenger) A messenger, standing between God and the human race, who is used to carry from God news of significance.

Anglican 40

Anglican Communion 40, 43, 45

Anglican Consultative Council 43

Anno Domini (see **A.D.**)

Annual Parochial Church Meeting (A.P.C.M.) 42, 44

Anointing 31, 32, 117, 133

Anointed One (see **Christ**)

Ante-Communion 7, 100, 106

Anthem 93

Antiphon 93

A.P.C.M. = Annual Parochial Church Meeting 42, 44

Apocalyptic (Greek – *apukalupsis* – uncovering of cf. Apocalypse) A word applied to writings in the Old and New Testaments* which are said to reveal things which are normally hidden, and to unveil the future. They often sprang out of conflict and persecution. The two prominent examples are the Book of Daniel* in the Old Testament and the Book of the Revelation of St John the Divine* in the New.

Apocrypha (Greek – *ta apokrupha* – the hidden things) The group of Biblical* books received by the early Church as part of the Greek version of the Old Testament*, but not included in the Hebrew Bible, being excluded by the non-Hellenistic (non Greek-speaking) Jews from their list of accepted books. The apocryphal books were written mostly during the 200 years before Christ. In most Bibles, they appear between the Old and New Testaments. In recent times they have become increasingly accepted as important historical source books, apart from their religious value.

Apologetics (Greek – *apologetikos* – reasoned defence) The defence of the Christian faith* on intellectual grounds by trained theologians* and philosophers.

Apostasy (Greek – *apostates* – deserter) The abandonment by a person of the Christian faith*.

Apostle

Apostle (Greek – *apostolos* – messenger) The title given in the Gospels* to the twelve chief disciples* of Christ and also, in the Book of the Acts* of the Apostles and the Epistles*, to Paul and Barnabas. In recent times the word has also come to be used of the first Christian missionary* to a country (e.g. Patrick, the Apostle of Ireland).

Apostles' Creed 18, 120

Apostolic (Greek – *apostolikos* – of a messenger) *Either* 'of the Apostles*' *or* 'derived from the Apostles' especially when applied to the Church*. The grace* and authority of Christ are held to descend through the Apostles, and their lawfully appointed successors.

Apparel 65

Apparitor (Latin – *apparere* – appear) An officer of an ecclesiastical* synod* or court.

Apse 77

Aramaic The Semitic language which was the language of the people of Palestine in the time of Christ* and which he himself almost certainly used. Examples to be found in the New Testament* are:
Abba – Mark*14.36 – 'Father'
Eloi, eloi, lama sabacthani – Mark 15.34 – 'My God, my God, why have you forsaken me?'
Ephphatha – Mark 7.34 – 'Be opened'
Maranatha – 1 Corinthians* 16.22 – 'O Lord, come'
Talitha kum – Mark 5.41 – 'Little girl, I tell you to get up'.

Arcade 77

Archangel (Greek – *arkhaggelos* – Chief angel*. In the Christian tradition, Michael, Gabriel and Raphael.

Archbishop 43, 50, 52, 54, 58, 59

Archbishops' Council 43

Archbishop's licence 117

Archdeacon 44, 50, 52, 55, 56, 57, 58, 59, 60, 61, 64

Archdeaconry 40, 50

Archdeacon's certificate 77

Arches, Dean of the 44, 57

Architecture – Saxon 70
Norman 71
Early English 72
Decorated 73
Perpendicular 74
Classical
revival 75
Gothic revival 76
Modern 76

Architrave 79

Area bishop 56

Area dean 55

Array, Lent 85, 99, 100

Arris 79

Articles of Enquiry (see **Articles of Visitation**)

Articles of Visitation 58, 64

Articles, Thirty-Nine 35

Ascension Day 11, 101

Ascription (Latin – *adscribere* – to write to) The words used at the end of a sermon* by a preacher* to give praise to God and to offer the sermon in his Name.

Ashlar 79

Ash Wednesday 99, 103

Asperges 107

Aspersion (Latin – *aspergere* – sprinkle) The method of baptism* whereby the candidate is sprinkled with the baptismal water* as opposed to affusion* or immersion*

Assistant Bishop 50

Athanasian Creed 120

Atonement (At-one-ment) The act of reconciling those at variance with each other – restoring a relationship broken by a wrong act. In Christian thinking, the reconciliation* of the human race with God through the sacrificial death of Christ. The author of the Letter to the Hebrews* was greatly influenced by the symbolism of the annual Jewish fast day, commonly called *Yom Kippur*, the purpose of which is the cleansing of the sanctuary, priesthood and people from sin* and the re-establishment of a proper relationship between God and his chosen ones. The writer of Hebrews saw Christ as the great High Priest whose Atonement on the Cross* abolished the need for the annual observance of the day.

At the Eucharist 105
Aumbry 79

Baldachino 79
Banner 78, 79
Banns of Marriage 117
Baptism 31, 32, 116
Baptismal ewer 83
Baptismal shell 79
Baptistery 79
Baroque 75
Barrel vault 79
Basilica 79
Bay 79
B.C. = Before Christ (see **A.D.**)
B.C.E. = Before the Common Era. It means time-wise, the same as B.C., but is deemed more acceptable to those of faiths other than Christian.
BCP = Book of Common Prayer
Beam, collar 79
Beam, hammer 79
Beam, tie 79
Beating of the Bounds A ceremony associated with the Rogationtide* procession* round the parish*. When parish boundary maps were unknown, this was a means of impressing the parish limits on the minds of the young. The bounds were solemnly beaten with willow rods. The custom still persists in some parishes.
Beatitudes (Latin – *beatitudo* – blessing) Christ's promises of coming blessings contained in Matthew* 5.3–11 (the Sermon

on the Mount) or Luke* 6.20–22 (the Sermon on the Plain). It is thought that the Beatitudes were a number of sayings spoken by Christ at different times, but collected together by the Gospel* writers and placed in a specific setting to give them more emphasis.
Beelzebub (Hebrew – *Baal-zebub* – lord of the flies. Greek – *Beelzebul*). Used in the Gospels* to denote the prince of devils.
Before Advent, Sundays 102
Before Christ (B.C.) (see **A.D.**)
Begotten (from beget) The word used in the *Gloria in excelsis** and the Nicene Creed* to emphasise that Christ, the eternal Son of God, could not have been made, created by the Father, but was 'of one being' with him. The distinction was made to combat the heresy* of Arius (see **Creeds** 120).
Belfry 79
Belial (Hebrew – *wickedness*) St.Paul uses the word of Satan*.
Bell, sanctus 114
Bell tower 79
Benedicite 94
Benediction (Latin – *benedictio* – blessing [literally to speak well of]). An alternative word for the blessing given at the end of services. Not to be confused with the service of Benediction*.
Benediction, service of 107
Benedictus 94
Benedictus qui 95
Benefice 41, 54, 58, 61, 63
Benefice, Union of, United 41
Bible/biblical (Greek – *biblion* – book – derived from *biblos* – papyrus bark) The Scriptures of the Old and New Testaments* as a book. Some Bibles also contain the Apocrypha* (see Section 12)
Bibles 135

Bidding Prayer A prayer* used publicly to call God's people to worship* (e.g. Morning and Evening Prayer* B.C.P.* and C.W.*) Bidding prayers of longer length are also used on special occasions (e.g. at the beginning of a festival of lessons* and carols*)

Bier 80

Biretta 65

Bishop 49, 116 *et passim*

Bishop, area 56

Bishop, assistant 50

Bishop, diocesan 52

Bishop, suffragan 55

Bishop's chaplain 50

Bishop's Council 46

Bishopric 59

Blasphemy (Greek – *blasphemia* – slander, damage to reputation) Speech, thought or action showing contempt for God.

Blessed Sacrament 79, 107, 114

Blessing 107

Book, altar 106

Book of Common Prayer (BCP) *passim*

Books, hymn 136

Books, Prayer 135

Boss 80

Both Kinds 107

Bounden (The old past participle of 'bind') The prayer which follows the Lord's Prayer in the BCP* Communion service contains the phrase 'our bounden duty'. It means 'that which we recognise and accept as a binding responsibility on our part'.

Bounds, Beating of the 5

Bowing 107

Box, confessional 82

Box, wafer 92

Brass 78, 80

Bread, unleavened 25, 114

Burial 119

Burse 107

Buttress 80

Buttress, flying 80

c. (Latin *circa*) approximately, about

Calendar 97, 98, 103

Calvary (Latin – *calvaria* – skull, Hebrew *Golgotha* – skull) The place of Christ's Crucifixion* just outside old Jerusalem.

Campanile 80

Candle, paschal 87, 100

Candlemas 102

Candlesnuffer 80

Canon, honorary 52

Canon law 43

Canon, minor 52

Canon missioner 50

Canon of the Mass 108

Canon of the Scriptures (Greek – *kanna* – reed or cane, measuring rod, *kanon* – rule, Latin – *scriptura* – writings) The list of books, officially received as inspired writings by the Church* and containing the rule of Divine Faith, which we now know as the Old and New Testaments* of the Bible*.

Canon, residentiary 55

Cantata 93

Canterbury cap 65

Canticle 93, 94

Cantor 93

Cantoris 93

Cantuar: The way in which the Archbishop* of Canterbury signs his official letters e.g. George Cantuar:. Cantuar: is a contraction of the Latin *Cantuariensis* which means 'of Canterbury'. Many bishops* sign in a similar manner e.g. the Archbishop of York = David Ebor:, the Bishop of Rochester = Michael Roffen:

Cap, Canterbury 65

Cap, college 66

Capital 80

Carol 93

Cartouche 80

Cassalb 65

Cassock 65

Catafalque 80

Catechism (Greek – *katekheo* – make hear and so instruct) A manual for use in the Church of England* by those seeking Confirmation*, which explains Christian doctrine* by question and answer method. There is a Catechism in the BCP*. A revised Catechism was published in 1961 and a further revision is planned.

Catechumen (Greek – *katekheo* – make hear and so instruct) In the early Church, a person undergoing training and instruction in preparation for Baptism.* The catechumens were dismissed from the Eucharist* at the end of the Ante-Communion*.

Cathedra 80

Cathedral 63, 80 (see **Dean**)

Cathedral chancellor 50

Catholic (Greek – *katholikos* – universally) In its primary meaning it denotes, when applied to the Church*, the idea of universality – the whole Church. It also implies the wholeness of Christian Truth.

Celebrant/celebrate 108

Cemetery 80

Censer 108

Ceremonial 108

Certificate, Archdeacon's 77

Cession 59

Chalice 108

Chancel 78, 80

Chancel step 78, 80

Chancellor, cathedral 50

Chancellor, Diocesan 56, 82

Chantry 80

Chantry chapel 81

Chapel 81

Chapel, chantry 81

Chapel, lady 78, 85

Chapel of ease 40

Chapel Royal 81

Chaplain 50

Chaplain, bishop's 50

Chaplain, college 50

Chaplain, embassy 50

Chaplain, examining 52

Chaplain, hospital 51

Chaplain, industrial 51

Chaplain, lay 57

Chaplain, nobleman's 51

Chaplain, prison 51

Chaplain, school 51

Chaplain to the Forces 50

Chaplain to the Sovereign 51

Chaplain, university 51

Chapter 40 *et passim*

Chapter Clerk *either* the (usually) lay* administrator on the staff of a cathedral* (see page 51) *or* a member of the clergy* who performs secretarial duties in a rural/area deanery* chapter (see page 40).

Chapter House 81

Charge 59

Charge, priest-in- 40, 41, 54

Charismata/charismatic (Greek – *kharismata*, plural of *kharisma* – a gift of grace*) The blessings bestowed by God on all Christians to enable them to fulfil the responsibilities of their calling. In the narrower sense, the word is used of the supernatural graces which individual Christians need to perform specific tasks within their calling. (See 1 Corinthians* 12.8–11) In recent years, the placing of a greater emphasis on the importance of the Charismata has led to the emergence of the Charismatic movement which reaches across the denominations*.

Charity (Latin – *caritas* – kindness. See also **agape**) The word has changed its meaning in modern usage. 'Charity' as used in e.g. the Authorised Version* of the Bible denoted the Christian virtue of 'love' – the translation now used in modern versions of the New Testament*. 'Charity' in modern usage denotes acts of kindness springing out of that love.

Chasuble 65, 67

Cherubim (Hebrew – *k'rubim*) The second of the nine orders of angels* whose particular gift was knowledge (see also **Seraphim**).

Chevron 81

Chimère 65

Chi Rho 98, 137

Choir (part of building) 78, 81

Choir (singers) 93

Choir habit 66

Choir Office 93

Chorister 93

Chrism 117

Christ (Greek – *khristos* – anointed one) The word is the Greek translation of the Hebrew word *mashah* – Messiah. It was originally a title used of Jesus, but soon came to be used by his followers as a proper name (e.g. Galatians* 1.3, Hebrews* 9.11). As a result they became known as Christians, as opposed to their earlier title of 'Followers of the Way'. The name serves to remind Christians that Jesus is indeed the Anointed One of God and the Messiah long-expected by the Jews. He is the fulfilment of God's revelation* in the Old Testament* – the One through whom God's will to reconcile* the human race to himself was achieved.

Christendom The Christian world. The word contains within itself a hope that, at some time in the future, the whole world will acknowledge the Lordship of Christ.

Christmas 98

Christmas Crib 81

Christmas Eve 98

Chronicles, First Book of 124

Chronicles, Second Book of 124

Church (building) 81

Church (institution) (Greek – *kuriakon* – belonging to the Lord – a word which was applied to a church building) The Latin *ecclesia* (which gives the modern word 'ecclesiastical'*) is derived from the Greek word *ekklesia*, which, although applied to the building, meant an assembly, primarily of citizens in a self-governing city. In its primary meaning, the 'Church' denotes all those, on earth and in heaven, who acknowledge Jesus as Lord – the assembly of the faithful. But it has taken on other secondary meanings, e.g. a building, a Communion (the Roman Catholic Church), the church of a defined area or country (the Church of England*), and is used as an adjective to describe those things or people who have to do with the Church (e.g. churchwarden*, churchyard*).

Church – architecture 70

    books 135

    contents 77

    creeds 120

    garments 65

    government 42

    ministers 48

    music 93

    organisation 40

    services 105, 116

    year 97

Church, collegiate 82

Church Commissioners 45

Church, daughter 41

Church, Guild 85

Church of England 40, 43–47 *et passim*

Church Overseas 40, 103

Church, parish 87

Church, priory 88

Church, redundant 62

Church Representation Rules 45

Churching of Women 119

Churchwarden 45, 46, 56, 63, 64

Churchwarden's stave 81

Churchyard 81

Ciborium 108

Cincture 65

Citation (Latin – *citare* – to set moving) A summons to appear before an ecclesiastical* court, or a legal document, usually affixed to a church* notice-board, giving notice of e.g.

intention to apply for a faculty* or intention to institute* to a benefice*

Classical revival architecture 75

Clerestory 81

Clergy 51

Clerical 51

Clerical wear 65

Clerk, Chapter 7

Clerk in Holy Orders 59

Clerk, lay 94

Clerk, parish 57

Cloak 65

Cloister 81

Cloth, altar 106

Cloth, fair linen 110

Collar beam 79

Collation 59

Collect 108

Collection 108

College cap 66

College chaplain 50

Collegiate church 82

Colonnade 82

Colossians, Letter to the 132

Colours, liturgical 97 *et passim*

Column 82

Column, engaged 83

Comfort (Latin – *fortis* – strong) 'Comfort', when used in the BCP*, denotes 'strength' or 'assurance', particularly when applied to the power of God's Holy Spirit*.

Comfortable Words 109

Comforter (Latin – *fortis* – strong) One who makes strong. (See also **Advocate**). A title of the Holy Spirit* (John 14.16 and 26, 15.26, 16.7).

Commemorations, Lesser Festivals and 102

Commissary (Latin – *committere* – to send) A representative of or deputy for a bishop*. Many overseas bishops have a commissary in Great Britain to represent their interests. If bishops are unable to be present at e.g. an institution*, they may appoint an assistant bishop as their commissary for the occasion.

Commissary court 82

Commissary General (see **Commissary court**)

Commissioners, Church 45

Committee, Standing 46

Common licence 117

Common Worship (C.W.) – *passim*

Communicant 109

Communion (a part of the Church) 40

Communion, Anglican 40, 43, 45

Communion Ante- 7, 100, 106

Compline 119

Concelebration 109

Concordance (Latin – *con* – with *cor, cordis* – heart – of one mind) A book of reference indicating all the passages of Scripture* in which a given word is found. The most famous concordance is that of Alexander Cruden, first published in 1737, but with many later editions.

Conference, Lambeth 46

Confession (faith) 109, 120

Confession (sin) 32, 82, 109, 118

Confession, Sacramental 26, 31, 32, 82, 118

Confessional box 82

Confirmation 31, 32, 48–49, 80, 116

Congregation (Latin – *grex, gregis* – flock, hence *congregare* – to flock together) A body of people assembled for religious worship*, or the term used to describe those who belong to a particular church.

Consecration (bishop) 48, 63

Consecration (church) 82

Consecration (elements) 109

Consistory Court 56, 82

Contemplation (Latin – *templum* – a place for observations) See **Prayer**

Contents, church 77

Contrition/contrite (Latin – *contritio* – a wearing away of something hard) Sorrow for sin* committed and determination to try to avoid further sin. A form of repentance*

Convent 59

Conventional District 40

Conversion (Latin – *convertere* – to turn about or round) The turning of sinners* to God through faith* in the saving power of Jesus Christ.

Convocation 44, 45

Convocation Dress 66

Convocation, Proctors in 42, 44

Cope 66

Corbel 82

Corinthians, First Letter to the 131

Corinthians, Second Letter to the 131

Coronation (Latin – *coronare* – to crown) see **The Sovereign**

Cornice 82

Corona 82

Corporal 109

Corpus Christi 103

Cotta 66

Council (Latin – *concilium* – assembly) Any ecclesiastical* assembly, but more particularly used to refer to the great Councils of the Church* before it became divided, the decisions of which are regarded as having great authority in the life of the Church. The first four General Councils of the Church – Nicaea, Constantinople, Ephesus and Chalcedon are accepted as authoritative by the Church of England*.

Council, Anglican Consultative 43

Council, Archbishops' 43

Council, Bishop's 46

Council, District Church 41, 45

Council, ecumenical (see **Council, Ecumenism**)

Council, Group 41

Council, Order in 46

Council, Parochial Church 41–46

Council, Team (see **Team Ministry**)

Course, string 91

Court, commissary 82

Court, consistory 56, 82

Covenant (Latin – *convenire* – to come together, agree) A bond entered into by two parties by which each is pledged to do something for the other. The idea of the covenant between the God of Israel and his people is fundamental to the religion of the Old Testament*. From the first it had ethical implications (see **Decalogue**). The earlier ideas of a covenant based on God leading the Israelites to victory over their enemies or ensuring good crops were developed during the time of the prophets* by their preaching that a true covenant with God depended on righteousness. Christ takes this idea a step further when he shows that in his life and death lies the perfect covenant between God and the human race which cannot achieve righteousness by its own efforts, i.e. solely by keeping a number of rules. It needs the free and undeserved gift of God's grace* to enable its righteousness to move towards perfection – and that perfection is seen only in Christ.

Covenant, local 61

Creator (Latin – *creator* – maker, founder) One of the titles of God, the Supreme Being, who is the universal creative force.

Credence (table) 78, 82

Credo 120

Creed – Apostles' 18, 120

Athanasian 120

Nicene 18, 105, 109, 120

Cremation 119

Crematorium 119

Crocket 82

Crosier 66, 68

Cross 78, 82, 100, 109, 116

Cross keys 137

Cross, pectoral 68

Cross, processional 88

Cross, sign of the 109
Cross, Stations of the 91
Crossing 83
Crucifix 78, 83
Crucifixion (Latin – *cruci fixus* – fixed to a cross) The act whereby Jesus Christ was put to death. Crucifixion was a penalty which arose in the East and was also frequently used by the Carthaginians. The Romans used it to put slaves to death, and, in some cases, those who could not prove Roman citizenship. It was preceded by whipping (scourging). The Emperor Constantine abolished crucifixion as a legal punishment in the 4th century (see also **Cross**).
Cruciform 83
Cruets 108, 109
Crypt 83
Curate 49, 51
Curate (old meaning) 51
Curate, perpetual 53
Cure 51, 59
Curtilage 83
C.W. = Common Worship, *passim*
Cusp 83

Daily office 118
Dalmatic 67
Daniel, Book of 127
Daughter church 41
Day, Lady 102
Day, Lammas 103
Day, Lord's 21
Day of Intercession (see Eve of St Andrew)
Days, Ancient of 3
Days, ember 102
Days, rogation 101
Days, special 102
Deacon (eucharist) 109
Deacon (order) 48, 51, 116
Deacon, sub 114
Dean 40, 50, 51–2
Dean, area 55
Dean of the Arches 44, 57
Dean, rural 55
Deanery 59

Deanery, rural *or* deanery 40, 42–44, 46
Deanery synod 42–46
Decalogue (Greek – *hoi deka logoi* – the ten words) The ten Commandments (Exodus* 20.1–17, Deuteronomy* 5.6–21). The body of religious and moral principles, based on the Hebrew conception of the one God. Apart from the commandments which prohibit the making of images and order the keeping of the sabbath*, they contain rules which are fundamental to the proper ordering of the life of society. Although in the Old Testament* the Commandments are given to Moses en bloc, it is generally believed that they emerged over a very long period as civilisation developed, and have been grouped together to give them an added impetus. The same is thought to be true of the Beatitudes* which are Christ's supplement to their teaching and are summed up in his two commands to love God and to love one's neighbour (Mark* 12.29–31).
Decani 93
Deceased (Latin – *decessus* – gone away) Dead
Decorated architecture 73
Dedication, Feast of 103
Deed of Relinquishment 59
Degrees of Affinity 2
Demythologisation (German – *Entmythologisierung*) – more correctly, remythologisation. An attempt to interpret the Scriptures* in forms acceptable to the people of today by eliminating the myths (e.g. belief in a three-storied universe – see **Ascension**) which were taken for granted by the Biblical* writers. The intention is to remove all extraneous material to allow a clearer and more realistic picture, particularly of

the 'actual' Christ, to emerge.

Denomination (Latin – *denominare* – to give a name to) The word used to describe the different sects within the Christian Church* e.g. Anglican*, Roman Catholic, Methodist, etc.

Deo, jubilate 95

Deuteronomy, Book called 122

Devil The (Greek – *diabolus* – slanderer, accuser) The chief of the fallen angels* and the cause of the sin* of the human race. In recent times there has been a move away from this traditional teaching. The Devil is now thought of more as a symbolic personalisation of evil, though Christians would not deny the presence of the forces of evil in the world (see **Satan**)

Devotion, The Three Hours' 119

Diaconate 48, 59

Diocesan bishop 52

Diocesan chancellor 56, 82

Diocesan synod 42–46

Diocese 40

Disciple (Latin – *discipulus* – one who learns from and is a follower of a leader) *Either* one of Christ's twelve Apostles*, *or* one of those who followed him in his lifetime, *or* any person who follows Christ.

Dish, lavabo 112

Dismissal 105, 109

Dissolution of the Monasteries Monasteries* had become an object of criticism in England in the later Middle Ages because of their enormous wealth and their moral laxity. But Henry VIII abolished the monastic system for personal motives. In 1536 he dissolved the smaller monasteries and in 1539 the larger monasteries. As a result he was able to replenish his depleted treasury and, at the same time, establish himself as supreme in Church* affairs. The Dissolution did not do as much social or economic harm as was at one time thought, but the losses to charity, art, learning, manuscripts and church furnishings were considerable (see **Reformation**).

District Church Council 41, 45

District, conventional 40

Divine Service 118

Divorcees, re-marriage of 117, 136

Doctrine (Latin – *docere* – to teach) The body of teaching which expresses the distinctive belief of a Church*. The Church of England* maintains that there are no distinctively Anglican* doctrines which are not doctrines of the whole Church.

Dogma (Greek – *dogma* – opinion – that which seems good) A religious truth established by God's revelation* and defined by the Church*.

D.O.M. 137

Dome 83

Dominical (Latin – *dominus* – Lord) Belonging to the Lord. It is used particularly of the two major sacraments*, Baptism* and the Lord's Supper* – sacraments which Christ himself instituted.

Dorsal 83

Dorter 83

Dove 137

Doxology 93

Drape 83

Dress, Convocation 66

Early English architecture 72

Ease, chapel of 40

Easter 97, 101, 136

Easter candle (see **Paschal candle**)

Easter Eve 100

Easter garden 83

Easter Week 101

Ecclesiastes, the Book called 125

Ecclesiastical (Greek – *ekklesia* – assembly) Matters concerning the Church* or the clergy*.

Ekklesia was the word used in early times by Greek-speaking Christians (see St Paul's letters*) to describe either a Christian community or the whole body of the Church.

Ecclesiology (Greek – *ekklesia* – assembly, *logos* – account) *Either* the science of the building or decoration of churches* *or* the doctrine* of the Church*.

Eclectic (Greek – *eklektikos* – picked out) Usually used of the congregation* of a parish church* whose members do not live in the parish concerned (e.g. city churches, where the population has moved away from the centre).

Ecumenical Council (see **Council**, **Ecumenism**)

Ecumenism (or Oecumenism) (Greek – *he oikoumene* – the whole inhabited earth) The movement in the Church* towards the recovery of the unity of all believers in Christ – 'that they may all be one' and the recognition that all things are united in Christ. In its early years, the movement sought the reunification of all Churches* into one body, with a consequent uniformity, but, in recent times, the emphasis has been placed on the maintenance of the separate traditions, but united in a common faith,* with the validity of the different ministries* acknowledged by all the Churches, and with Baptism* and the Eucharist* as the central unifying features shared by all. (Adjective – Ecumenical) The principal ecumenical body is the World Council of Churches, and is supported by national bodies, e.g. Churches Together in England, etc., and similar bodies at local level.

Effigy 83

Elections 42, 44

Electoral Roll 42, 43, 57

Elements 109

Elevation (architecture) 83

Elevation (liturgical) 109

Elohim (Hebrew – 'gods') Used occasionally in the Old Testament* to describe heathen gods, but generally of the God of Israel. The Pentateuch* emerged from several sources before being edited into its present form. These sources are identified by initial letters by Biblical scholars. Those parts of the Pentateuch which use 'Elohim' as the name for God are known as 'E' sources (see also **Jehovah**).

Embassy chaplain 50

Ember days 102

Emeritus (Latin – past participle of *Emereri* – to earn) retired and retaining one's title as an honour e.g. dean* emeritus.

Emmanuel (Hebrew – 'with us (is) God') Isaiah*7.14 and 8.8. The word has several interpretations, but in Matthew*1.23, the prophecy* is interpreted with reference to the birth of Christ*.

Empty Tomb (see **Easter**)

Endowments 46

Engaged column 83

Enquiry, articles of (see **Articles of Visitation**)

Entablature 83

Enthronement, Enthronization 59

Ephesians, Letter to the 131

Epiklesis 109

Epiphany 98

Episcopal 59

Episcopate 59

Epistle 105, 110, 130–133

Epistoler 110

Eschatology (Greek – *eskhatos* – last, *logos* – word) A theological* term used to denote the final destiny both of the individual soul* and of the human race in general – what is yet to happen at the end of human history – often called 'the last things'. In the Old Testament*, eschatology is closely bound up with the hope of the coming of the Messiah*. In the New Testament*, it is the subject of many of our Lord's parables (e.g. Tares among the Wheat **Matthew*** 13.25 and the Drag Net **Matthew*** 13.47). It is frequently mentioned by St Paul* (especially 1st and 2nd Thessalonians*) and is the main subject of the apocalypses in the Book of the Revelation* (see **Apocalyptic**).

Eschew (BCP* Collect* for Easter 3) An old word meaning 'avoid' or 'reject'.

Establishment (see **Reformation**)

Esther, the Book of 124

Eternal (see **Temporal**)

Eucharist 31, 32, 94, 95, 100, 105

Eucharist, At the 105

Eucharist, music for the 95

Eulogy (Greek – *eulogia* – praise) An address given at a funeral* in praise of a deceased* person.

Evangelical 62

Evangelism (Greek – *euaggelistes* – one who spreads good news) The preaching* of the Gospel* whereby people come to accept Jesus Christ as Lord and Saviour*.

Evangelist (Greek – *euaggelistes* – one who spreads good news) *Either* a title given to the authors of the four Gospels* *or* one who preaches and teaches the Gospel.

Eve, Christmas 98

Eve, Easter 100

Eve of St Andrew 103

Evening Prayer 119

Evensong 119

Ewer, baptismal 83

Examining chaplain 52

Exodus, the Book of the 122

Ex-officio 46

Exorcism/Exorcist (Greek – *ex* -out, *orkizo* – use an oath) The practice of expelling evil spirits by calling upon the name of Jesus Christ* and with prayer*

Expiation (Latin – *piare* – seek to appease, make amends for) Making amends for an offence committed against God or one's neighbour. The only perfect expiation of human sin* is Christ's* offering of his earthly life and death.

Exposition 110

Extempore prayer (Latin – *ex tempore* – on the spur of the moment) Spoken prayer* made without notes or preparation.

Extreme unction (see **Anointing**)

Ezekiel, Book of the Prophet 127

Ezra, the Book of 124

Faculty 56, 83

Fair linen cloth 110

Faith (Latin – *fides* – faith) *Either* the body of truth (the Christian faith) to be found above all in the revelation* of God contained in the Bible* and also in the Creeds*, the definitions of the great Councils* of the Church*, and the teachings of the Church's saints* and teachers. *Or* the human response to Divine truth and, springing from that, a trusting dependence on the God revealed in that truth and a grateful acceptance of all that God's love has achieved for the human race in the Death and Resurrection* of Christ.

Faldstool 84

Fall, pulpit 88

Fall, The The term used to denote the reality that the human race, although created in the image of God for fellowship with him, has fallen short of that destiny and become sinful*. The Fall is presented symbolically in the Old Testament* book of Genesis* by the story of Adam and Eve in the Garden of Eden.

Fan vault 84

Fast 99, 110

Father 60

Feast (Latin – *festus* – joyous) A joyful religious anniversary. See Festivals.

Feast of Dedication 103

Feasts, movable 104

Fees, surplice 63

Feet, washing of (see **Maundy Thursday**)

Fellowship One of the distinguishing marks of the Christian community is its quality of fellowship (Greek *koinonia*). It is a community bound together in love by a common dedication to our Lord and his service. Paul* describes it as 'the Fellowship of the Holy Spirit*' (2 Corinthians* 13.14).

Feretory 84

Ferial 110

Festival, patronal 103

Festivals and Principal Holy Days 98–103

Festivals, Lesser 102

Filioque (Latin – 'and the Son') The clause in the Nicene Creed* – C.W.* 'We believe in the Holy Spirit* . . . who proceeds from the Father *and the Son*' – (cf. John*16.13–15). Added by the Western Church* to that creed at the Third Council* of Toledo in A.D.* 589. The Orthodox* Church regards its addition as unacceptable, because it believes there can only be a single Fount of Divinity in the Godhead*.

Fillet 84

Finial 84

Fish 137

Flag 84

Flagon 110

Flèche 84

Floor, ringing 89

Flute 84

Flying buttress 80

Font 78, 84

Forces, Chaplain to the 50

Forgiveness (Old English – *forgiefan*) In the Christian sense, the pardoning of sin* by God made possible by Christ's victory over evil on the Cross*. Springing out of that, an essential part of the Christian life is that, as God forgives us, so we should forgive those who sin against us.

Foundation, New 52, 53

Foundation, Old 50, 53, 54, 56

Fraction 110

Freehold 60

Friar 52

Friary 60

Friday, Good 100

Frontal 84

Fundamentalism (Latin – *fundamentum* – foundation) The Protestant* movement which, amongst other distinctive doctrines*, emphasises the supreme authority of the Bible* and the need for strict orthodoxy* in the matter of Biblical interpretation, accepting the text as literally true in every respect.

Funeral 119, 138

Galatians, the Letter to the 131

Galilee 84

Gallery 84

Gargoyle 84

Gate, lych 86

Gehenna (Hebrew – *Gehinnom* – hell) The Valley of Hinnom, running SW to S of Jerusalem. From early times, it was a place of human sacrifice where fires burned constantly and there is some evidence that it later became a place for the destruction of rubbish. It was seen by Old Testament* writers as a divinely-appointed place of punishment. In the New Testament*, Gehenna is used as a symbolic object lesson to the wicked to warn them that the final place of torment after the Last Judgement* will be similar (see also **Hell**).

General Synod 42–46

General Thanksgiving B.C.P.*
Thanksgivings, C.W.* *Sunday Service Book* Prayers for Various Occasions. A prayer composed by Bishop* Reynolds in 1661. It was named 'general' to distinguish it from the 'particular' thanksgivings (e.g. for rain) which follow in the B.C.P.

Genesis, the Book called 121

Gentile (Latin – *gentiles* – foreigners) The word usually applied by Jews to any person not a Jew

Genuflection 110

Ghost, Holy 17, 102

Girdle 67

Glass, stained 90

Glebe 54, 60

Gloria in Excelsis Deo 95

Gloria Patri 95

Glory (Latin – *gloria* – glory) *Either* the revealing of God's presence, especially in Jesus Christ, *or* the giving of honour to God.

Godhead The being and nature of God.

God-parent 116

Good Friday 100

Gospel (Old English – *god spel* – good tidings) *Either* the Good News of the Kingdom of God preached by Jesus Christ *or* one of the four Gospels (Matthew*, Mark*, Luke*, John*) appearing in the New Testament* *or* the passage from one of the Gospels read at the Eucharist*.

Gospeller 110

Gothic Revival Architecture 76

Governance (Latin – *gubernare* – steer, govern) (BCP* Morning Prayer* 3rd Collect*, Collect for Trinity 5) An old word used of God's authority as expressed through his will.

Government and Representation, Church 42–47

Grace (Latin – *gratia*, – Greek – *charis* – favour freely shown, especially by a superior to an inferior) The favour and kindness of God, freely shown to the human race in the life and death of his Son, in spite of it being undeserving of it because of its sinfulness*. It is the saving activity of the divine love, freely given and able to be shared by those who recognise their need for forgiveness*.

Grace at meals The custom of giving thanks in prayer* before and after meals. (cf. John* 6.11, Acts 27.35)

Grace, The 35

Gradual 110

Gradual hymn 93

Grave 119

Groin 84

Group Council (see **Group ministry**)

Group ministry 41

Guild Church 85

Habbakuk, Book of the Prophet 128

Habit 67

Habit, choir 66

Hades (Greek) The place or state of departed spirits – not hell*. Apostles' Creed* – B.C.P.* 'He descended into hell', C.W.* (contemporary language version) 'He descended to the dead'.

Haggai, Book of the Prophet 129

Hallelujah see **Alleluia**

Hallow (German – *heilig* – holy) *Either* to honour as holy *or* to make holy. The word is used in the first sense in the Lord's Prayer. 'Hallow' in the second sense is not much used. It is an old word for 'saint'*, i.e. one who is 'made holy' – accepted by the Church* as a person worthy of the title. All Hallows' is an alternative name for All Saints' Day (November 1st).

Hallows, All (see **Hallow**)

Halo (Greek – *halos* – disc of sun or moon) A circle or disc of light usually round the head – used by the Greeks as a symbol of the gods and by the Romans of their god-emperors. It was taken over gradually by Christian art, first for Christ* and the Blessed Virgin Mary, then for angels*, saints* and other important people. Also known as a nimbus.

Hammer beam 79

Hands, laying on of see **Ministry to the Sick**

Harvest Thanksgiving 103

Hassock 85

Hatchment 85

Healing Ministry (see **Ministry to the Sick**)

Hearse (Medieval Latin – *erpica*) A vehicle for carrying a coffin* at a funeral*.

Heaven Our understanding of the word 'heaven' will not be helped if we attempt to talk in terms of a place or a state. The idea of 'heaven' being 'above the bright blue sky' had its origins in the Jewish concept of the universe (see Section 8: **Ascension**). Jesus makes it quite clear that heaven is with us already even before we experience death. It is the goal of perfection, already there in God, but also something towards which we can strive. It is therefore the eternal Presence of God, into which we hope to come in the life beyond the grave, but of which we can be aware in this present life.

Hebrews, Letter to the 132

Hell (see also **Gehenna**) The lurid ideas of Hell as the place of eternal punishment now carry little conviction. The word becomes meaningful if we think of it more in terms of 'separation from God' – a state into which God's children place themselves by the wilful and ultimate act of rejecting his love.

Heresy (Greek – *hairesis* – choice or sect) An opinion contrary to the orthodox* doctrine* of the Christian Church* (see Section 11).

Hermit/ hermitage (Greek – *eremia* – desert) One who, from religious motives, has chosen to live a solitary life.

Hierarchy (Greek – *hieros* – sacred, *arkhe* – rule) The ordered levels of authority in the structure of the Church*, often used to describe the higher levels of authority.

High altar 85

High mass 110

Holiday 103

Holy/holiness (see **Sanctification**)

Holy Communion 31, 32, 47, 95, 100, 111

Holy Days, Principal 96–103

Holy Ghost/Holy Spirit (see also **Advocate**) The third Person of the Trinity*. In sixteenth and seventeenth century English, the word 'ghost' (German – *Geist*) meant 'spirit', whether of God or of a human being. Because, in later times, 'ghost' took on a more restricted meaning, viz. someone returned from the dead to haunt people or places, the word 'Spirit' is now more commonly used when referring to the third Person of the Trinity. The Holy Spirit is distinct from but consubstantial, coequal and coeternal with the Father and the Son, and, in the fullest sense, God. He works extensively in the world and intensively in the Church*. He is the Sanctifier*, the one who makes holy the people of God (see also 102).

Holy Orders 31, 32, 48, 49, 116

Holy Saturday (see **Easter Eve**)

Holy Spirit (see **Holy Ghost**)

Holy table 85

Holy Week 100, 136

Homily (Greek – *homileo* – hold converse) A sermon* with emphasis on spiritual teaching.

Homoousion (Greek – of one substance, consubstantial) The term used in the Nicene Creed* to express the relation of the Father and the Son within the Godhead*. It was introduced to combat the heresy* of Arianism. B.C.P* 'of one substance with the Father', C.W.* 'of one Being with the Father'.

Honorary canon 52

Hood 67

Hosanna (Hebrew – *hosha'na* – save, pray) The word means 'Save, we pray you' and was used by the crowds when they proclaimed Jesus to be the Messiah (see **Christ**) on his triumphal entry into Jerusalem on Palm Sunday*. The word was taken into Christian worship from a very early date, and, paradoxically, now has an overtone of joy.

Hosea, Book of the Prophet 127

Hospital chaplain 51

Host 111

Hosts, Lord God of (see **Sabaoth**)

House, chapter 81

Humble Access, Prayer of 111

Hymn, gradual 93
introit 94
offertory 94
office 94
processional 94

Hymn books 136

Icon 85

Icthus 137

I.H.S. 138

Image (Latin – *imago Dei* – image of God) Genesis* 1.26 tells us that the human race was created in the image of God. It is part of God's total creation but also unique. It is the image of God which distinguishes its members from the rest of creation, but the Bible* does not define clearly its nature or where it is found. Scholars see this image as lying in several areas – in freewill, in reason, in part in moral nature, thirst for God, and creative abilities.

Immanence (Latin – *in* – in, *manere* – to remain) The word denotes the belief that God is everywhere present in his creation, but is always coupled in Christian thought with the further belief that he is also transcendent (see **Transcendence**).

Immersion (Latin – past participle of *immergere* = *immersum*) A method of baptism* whereby part of the candidate's body is submerged whilst the baptismal water is poured over the remainder. To be distinguished from submersion or 'total immersion'. (See also **Affusion, Aspersion**.)

Impediment (Latin – *impedimentum* – obstacle, hindrance) In canon* law, an obstacle standing in the way of a properly constituted marriage* B.C.P.* – rubrics* re the calling of banns* – 'if any of you know cause or just impediment why these two persons should not be joined together in Holy Matrimony*, ye are to declare it'. C.W.* *Pastoral Services* (marriage) 'If any of you know any reason in law etc.'

Imposition (Latin – *imponere* – place on) A word used to describe the laying on of the bishop's* hands in, for example, Confirmation*, Ordination*.

Incarnate/Incarnation (Latin – *incarnare* – to become flesh) Apostles' Creed* (C.W.*) 'he was conceived by the power of the Holy Spirit, born of the Virgin Mary'. Nicene Creed* (C.W.*) 'was incarnate from the Holy Spirit and the Virgin Mary.' The Christian faith affirms that the eternal Son of

God took human flesh from his human mother and that this same Jesus, who lived at a particular point in history, is, at one and the same time, fully God and fully man.

Incense 111

Incorporate (Latin – *corpus* – body – be part of) In the Christian sense, spiritually to be part of Christ's Body, and, by extension, part of his Church*.

Incumbent 60

Indifferent The word has changed its meaning. 'Indifferent to' now generally means 'lacking interest in', whereas formerly it meant 'impartial' – lacking in bias and therefore 'fair'.

Induction 50, 60

Industrial chaplain 51

Inhibition 60

Iniquity (Latin – *in* – un, *iquus* – just) Wickedness

I.N.R.I. 138

Institution The word has many meanings, the most important of which are mentioned elsewhere in the text, e.g. the Institution of the Holy Communion* by our Lord at the Last Supper*, the institution of an incumbent* to the spiritual care of a living, and the Church* as an institution.

Institution, words of 100, 111

Intercession 111

Intercession, Day of (*see* **Eve of St Andrew**)

Interment 119

Interregnum 60

Intinction 111

Intone 93

Introit 111

Introit hymn 94

Invocation (Latin – *invocare* – call) To call upon somebody to do something. From earliest days, Christians have invoked the help of the Holy Spirit*. In some parts of the Church*, invocation is used in the sense of asking the Blessed Virgin Mary,

the mother of our Lord, and the saints* for their prayers.

Isaiah, Book of the Prophet 125

James, the Letter of 133

Jehovah The anglicised version of the Hebrew word for 'God' (see **Yahweh**). Those sources in the Pentateuch* which use *Yahweh* as the name for 'God' are known as 'J' documents (see **Deuteronomy, Elohim**).

Jeremiah, the Book of the Prophet 126

Jesse window 85

Jesus (The Greek form *Iesous* of the Hebrew Joshua = '*Yahweh* (Jehovah) saves') The name bestowed on the infant Christ by divine command (Luke* 1.31, Matthew* 1.21). The name effectively describes the purpose of Christ's work – the salvation* of the human race.

Job, Book of 124

Joel, Book of the Prophet 127

John, Gospel according to 130

John, First Letter of 133

John, Second Letter of 133

John, Third Letter of 133

Jonah, Book of 128

Joshua, Book of 122

Jubilate Deo 95

Jude, the Letter of 133

Judgement (Latin – *jus* – right, *dicus* – speaking) The Last or General Judgement is, in Christian thought, the final judgement on the human race after the Resurrection* of the Dead on the 'Last Day'. It is held to be the occasion of God's final sentence on humanity as a whole, as well as his verdict on both the soul* and body of each individual. The Particular Judgement is held to be God's verdict on individual souls at the moment of death. All people are accountable to God for their stewardship of the lives he gives them. His verdict on that stewardship will always be tempered by mercy*, in the light of his revelation* of himself, in Christ, who came not to destroy but to fulfil.

Judges, Book of the 123

Justification (Latin – *justum facere* – to make just) Christian teaching is that the human race is not, by nature, righteous, but sinful*. It stands, therefore, not in a right, but in a wrong relationship to God, and cannot of itself put this right. The relationship can only be restored by finding pardon and acceptance with God through God's grace*. In Protestant* theology*, justification is seen as the act whereby God, in virtue of the Sacrifice of Christ, acquits individuals of the punishment due to their sins and, in his mercy*, treats them as though they were righteous. According to Martin Luther, this justification was granted to the sinner only in response to the disposition of faith* (Latin – *sola fides*).

Kerygma (Greek – *kerugma* – preaching) The element of proclamation in the Gospel* as opposed to its teaching content.

Keys, cross 137

Kinds, both 107

Kingdom of God The theme of the Kingdom of God (or, in St Matthew's Gospel*, Heaven*) is central to the message of the New Testament*. John the Baptist saw its coming as an imminent event. Jesus Christ changed the concept prevailing at his time by making it clear that entrance into the Kingdom was not to be a political affair achieved by the military overthrow of the nations. Rather, entrance into the Kingdom would depend on the moral and religious qualities of those seeking it. So, in a real sense, it would be possible for believers to enjoy the Kingdom in the present, though its final consummation would be in the future. Although the link between the Kingdom and God's community, the Church*, was not made in the New Testament, later scholars saw it as self-evident.

Kings, the First Book of 123

Kings, the Second Book of 123

King post 85

Kiss of peace 105, 111

Kneel (Old Saxon – *knio*) Resting on the knees is a widely used Christian practice when praying*.

Kneeler (see **Hassock**)

Kyrie eleison 96

Lady chapel 78, 85

Lady Day 102

Laity 56, 57

Lamb, paschal 122, 138 (see also **Passover**)

Lambeth Conference 46

Lamentations, the Book of 126

Lammas Day 103

Lancet 85

Lantern 85

Lapsed (Latin – *lapsus* – fallen) Those who have fallen away from the Faith*

Laud (Latin – *laus* – praise) Praise (also laudable, praiseworthy) BCP* Communion Service, 'We laud and magnify thy holy name'. ['Lauds' was one of the ancient offices of the Church.]

Lavabo dish 112

Lavabo towel 112

Law, canon 43

Lay 57

Lay chaplain 57

Lay clerk 94

Lay rector 54, 57

Laying on of hands A sign of blessing (e.g. at Ordination* or Confirmation*) giving assurance of

God's favour. The laying on of hands is now also an accepted part of the Church's* healing ministry (see **Ministry to the Sick**)

Leaven (Latin – *levare* – lift) An old word for 'yeast', the material which helps fermentation, especially in dough. The word is used symbolically in the New Testament* not only to illustrate the dynamic effect of the Good News on those who follow Christ, but also to illustrate the damage done by the leaven of malice and wickedness.

Lectern 78, 85
Lectionary 103
Lent 99, 136
Lent array 85, 99, 100
Lesser festivals 102
Lesson, Lection (Latin – *lectio* – reading) A passage of Scripture* read aloud at divine service*.
Letters dimissory 60
Letters of Orders 61
Letters, Pastoral 132
Letters, St Paul's 130–132
Leviticus, the Book called 122
Licence, archbishop's 117
Licence, common 117
Lierne vaulting 85
Light 85
Lights, sanctuary 89
Lintel 85
Litany 119
Literate 61
Liturgical colours 97 *et passim*
Liturgy 112
Living (see **Quick**)
Local covenant 61
Loft, rood 89
Logos (Greek – *logos* – word or reason) 'The Word' -a title of Christ used particularly in the writings of John* (Especially John 1.1 & 14). Heraclitus (c. 500 B.C.) used the word to describe the universal reason governing and permeating the world. In the Old Testament*, God's word was not only his

means of communicating with the human race, but also the expression of his creative power. Philo, a Jewish thinker (c. A.D. 20), saw the Logos as the divine pattern from which the material world is copied, the divine power in the cosmos, the divine purpose or agent in creation and an intermediary between God and the human race. John was clearly influenced by Philo's school of thought, but added an extra concept by identifying the Logos with the Messiah* (see **Christ**).

Lord of Hosts (see **Sabaoth**)
Lord's Day A name for Sunday* (see **Revelation*** 1.10)
Lord's Prayer (see **Prayer**)
Lord's Supper 112
Love (Greek – *agape*, Latin – *caritas*) In Christian thought, the essential quality underlying God's actions and our response to them. It is distinguished from the Greek *philia* – dutiful affection and *eros* – passionate emotion, and is seen more as a matter of the will than of the emotions. It is selflessness from which the element of sacrifice is never far removed. For Christ, love was the basis of his commandments – love God, love your neighbour.

Low mass 112
Low Sunday 101
Lozenge 85
Luke, Gospel according to 130
Lych-gate 86

Magi (Old Persian – *magus*, Greek – *magos* – *either* a member of an ancient Persian priestly caste *or* a sorcerer) (see **Epiphany**)
Magnificat 95
Malachi, the Book called 129
Mammon (Aramaic – *mamon* – riches) Wealth which becomes an idol and excludes love of God (Matthew* 6.24).

Manifest (BCP*) Seen clearly.

Manifold (BCP*) Many and various.

Maniple 67

Manual acts 112

Mark, Gospel according to 130

Marriage 31, 32, 117

Marriage, banns of 117

Martyr (Greek – *martus* – witness) One who undergoes the penalty of death for witnessing to Christ or the Christian faith*.

Mass 112

Mass, canon of the 108

Mass, high 110

Mass, low 112

Mass, nuptial 112

Mass of the Presanctified 112

Mass, proper of the 113

Mass, requiem 113

Matthew, Gospel according to 130

Mattins 118

Matrimony (see **Marriage**)

Maundy Thursday 100

Mediator (Latin – *medius* – middle, so one who stands in the middle) A mediator is one who stands between two parties and whose function is to reconcile. The word is used of the work of Christ in reconciling the human race to God (see **Reconciliation**).

Meditation (Latin – *meditari* – frequent) (see **Prayer**)

Meet An old word which means 'the proper thing to do' (e.g. BCP* Communion service – 'it is meet and right so to do'.)

Meeting, Annual Parochial Church 42, 44

Memorial (Latin – *memor* – mindful) – also 'memory' 'remembrance'. The celebration of the Eucharist* is sometimes referred to as a 'memorial' of Christ's Cross* and Passion*. It is important to remember that, in Jewish thought, a 'memorial' not only meant a remembering of an event in the past, but also

a re-enacting of that event in the present – a calling into the present of the reality and the benefits of that past event. This, then, makes of the Eucharist a constant reminder of what our Lord did at the Last Supper (see Section 8: **Maundy Thursday**), but also serves to assure those who take part in it of its reality and its benefits for them in the present. Through the bread* and the wine*, symbols of our Lord's Body and Blood, they enter into the Real Presence of Christ.

Mensa 86

Mercy (Latin – *merces* – reward) Applied to God, 'mercy' refers to his work, not only in creation, revelation* and the care of the human race, but more particularly in its redemption* through our Lord Jesus Christ. God's mercy is his free and gracious loving-kindness, unmerited and undeserved.

Merit (Latin – *meritus* – earned, deserved) BCP* Communion service – 'by the merits of the most precious death and passion* of thy dear Son'. The blessings won for the human race by the sacrifice of Christ.

Messiah (see **Christ**)

Metropolitan 52

Micah, Book of the Prophet 128

Michaelmas 103

Militant (Latin – *militare* – to fight) BCP* Communion service – 'the Church militant here in earth'. The Church* is engaged in a continuing militant struggle against the forces of evil. The final victory in that struggle has not yet been achieved. When the day comes on which all will recognise the sovereignty of God and the Lordship of Christ, the Church militant will become the Church triumphant.

Mind, Year's 38
Minister 61
Minister, non-stipendiary 53
Minister, sector 55
Ministry 48
Ministry, group 41
Ministry, healing (see **Ministry to the Sick**)
Ministry, sacred 62
Ministry, team 41
Ministry to the Sick 113, 117, 119, 136
Minor canon 52
Minster 86
Miracle (Latin – *miraculum* – a wonderful thing) A perceivable happening produced for a religious end by the special intervention of God which transcends (see **Transcendence**) the normal order of things, i.e. the Law of Nature.
Misericord 86
Missal 112
Mission/Missionary (Latin – *mittere* – send) The Mission of the Church* is to bring all people to Christ. The Apostles*, and all those who have followed them, believed that Christ sent them out into the world to achieve this aim. Missionaries are men and women who believe they are called by him to take the Good News of the Gospel* to those who have not heard it. Although missionaries have been largely involved in fulfilling this aim in countries overseas, it is obvious that any initiative taken to bring a person to Christ, whether at home or overseas, is part of the Church's Mission.
Missioner, canon 50
Mitre 68
Modern architecture 76
Monasteries, dissolution of the 12, 29, 52, 53
Monastery 61
Monk 52
Monograms, sacred 137

Monstrance 112
Monument 86
Morning Prayer 119
Mortify (Latin – *mortificare* – to put to death) Used figuratively to denote the act of consciously rejecting the evils by which the Christian's relationship with God is spoiled.
Motet 94
Mothering Sunday 99
Movable Feasts 104
Mullion 86
Music, church 93
Music for the Eucharist 95
Mystery/Mysteries (Greek – *musterion* – something hidden) In the Bible*, the word 'mystery' is used in a distinctive way – either to denote the plan of God, his purpose in history, his eternal purpose and sovereignty or to denote the medium through which the secret plan of God is disclosed. Christ fulfils both these definitions. He is the perfect unique medium by which the purpose of God in history has been disclosed. He is the 'open secret' of God.
  The word 'mysteries' or 'sacred mysteries' is often used to describe the Body and Blood of Christ given in the Communion*, or of the service itself.

Nahum, Book of the Prophet 128
Narthex 86
Nave 78, 87
Nave altar 87
Nehemiah, the Book of 124
New Foundation 52, 53
Nicene Creed 18, 105, 109, 120
Nimbus (see **Halo**)
Nobleman's chaplain 51
Non-stipendiary minister 53
Norman architecture 71
North side 112
Novena (Latin – *novem* – nine) A period of nine days' private or public prayer* by which it is

hoped to obtain some special grace* or to influence a course of action.

Novice 53

Numbers, the Book called 122

Numinous (Latin – *numen* – a local god) What is experienced in religion* as 'the holy*'. It will call forth feelings of awe, self-abasement and fascination from the individual.

Nun 53

Nunc Dimittis 95

Nunnery 61

Nuptial Mass 112

Obadiah, the Book of the Prophet 128

Oblations 112

Occasional Offices 119

Octave 104

Offertory 112

Offertory hymn 94

Office (Latin – *officium* – office) *Either* a position with duties attached to it e.g. the office of a priest*, *or* the authorised form of daily worship*, *or* the divine service* which gives effect to this.

Office, choir 93

Office, daily 118

Office hymn 94

Office of Reception (see **Reception, office of**)

Offices, occasional 119

Official Principal (see **Chancellor, Diocesan**)

Oil 31, 32, 117, 133

Old Foundation 50, 53, 54, 56

Old Testament lesson 105, 113

Omnipotence (Latin – *omnis* – all, *potens* – be able) The infinite power of God.

Omnipresence (Latin – *omnis* – all, *praesens* – be at hand) The infinite presence of God.

Omniscience (Latin – *omnis* – all, *scientia* – knowledge) The infinite knowledge of God.

Oratorio 94

Oratory 87

Ordain/Ordination 31, 32, 48, 49, 61, 117

Order, religious 62

Order in Council 46

Orders 48

Orders, clerk in holy 59

Orders, letters of 61

Ordinal 61, 116

Ordinand 61

Ordinary 61

Organ/Organist 78, 87

Organisation 40

Original sin (Latin – *sous* – guilty) The state when the human race separates itself from God by its unbelief and pride, as opposed to the acts of sin which follow from that revolt (see **Sin**).

Orphrey 68

Orthodox/Orthodoxy (Greek – *orthos* – straight, *doxa* – opinion) Orthodoxy is the holding of correct or currently accepted opinions in matters of religious doctrine*, as opposed to heresy*. The Orthodox Church* is the Eastern or Greek Church which recognises the Patriarch of Constantinople as its head.

Other services 116

Our Father The first two words of the Lord's Prayer. See **Prayer**.

Padre 61

Pagan (Latin – *paganus* – from *pagus* – country district) An unenlightened person. One who does not believe in God.

Pall 113

Palm Sunday 99

Panegyric (Greek – *panegurikos* – of public assembly) A speech given publicly in praise of a person particularly when deceased*.

Parable (Greek – *parabole* – a story to teach a lesson) A distinctive feature of Christ's teaching. The parables are likenesses drawn from nature or human affairs which Christ used to convey a spiritual meaning.

Many of them are to do with the Kingdom of God*, and many of them were warnings to the Jews of his day that their status as the chosen people of God was being put in jeopardy by their unwillingness to listen to the Good News Christ came to bring.

Paraclete (Greek – *parakletos* – advocate) A title of the Holy Spirit (see **Advocate**).

Parclose 87

Parent, god 116

Parish 40

Parish church 87

Parish clerk 57

Parish priest 53

Parishioner (Greek – *paroikos* – dwelling) An inhabitant of a parish*.

Parochial 61

Parochial Church Council (P.C.C.) 41–46

Parousia (Greek – *parousia* – presence or arrival) The future return of Christ in glory* (the Second Coming) to judge the living and the dead, and to terminate the present world order. Early Christians (see **1 & 2 Thessalonians***) believed that Christ's return was imminent. Some scholars hold that Nero's persecution of the Christians after the fire at Rome (AD 64) was due to their thinking that the fire was a sign that the Parousia had begun. Because of this, they came out into the open and suffered accordingly. Christian tradition today, although maintaining that there will be a General Judgement (see **Judgement**) which will mark the end of the present order, is not prepared to speculate about the exact time and manner of the Coming.

Parson 61

Parsonage 61

Parvis 87

Paschal candle 87, 100

Paschal lamb (see **Passover**)

Passion, Passion Sunday 99

Passover The Jewish festival celebrated every spring in connection with the Exodus. According to the account of its institution in Exodus* 12, a lamb is to be slain in each household and its blood sprinkled on the lintel and doorposts of the house in memory of the fact that, when the firstborn of Egypt were slain, the Lord 'passed over' the houses so marked. The eating of the Paschal Lamb* was associated with the use of unleavened bread*. The Eucharist* was instituted by Christ at Passover time, and Christian writers, from St Paul* onwards, have stressed that the death of Christ was the fulfilment of the sacrifice foreshadowed by the Passover. (See also Section 6: **Paschal candle**, Section 8: Introduction, Section 9: **Unleavened bread**, Section 14: **Paschal Lamb**, and in Section 12: **Exodus**).

Pastor (Latin – *pastor* – shepherd) For Christ, his care for his followers was like that of a shepherd for his flock. Pastors are those who exercise that care on behalf of Christ, e.g. parish priests* ministering to their congregations*. Bishops* are often described as the chief pastors in their dioceses*. Adjective: pastoral.

Pastoral staff (see **Crosier**)

Pastoral Letters (see **1 Timothy***, **2 Timothy***, **Titus***) 132

Paten 113

Patron/Patronage 61

Patron Saint The saint after whom a church is named.

Patronal festival 103

Paul, St 130

Pax 113

P.C.C. = Parochial Church Council

Penance (Latin – *paenitentia* – being sorry) An act carried out by a penitent* to demonstrate the sincerity of the penitence*. The word is also used to describe Sacramental Confession*.

Penitence (Latin – *paenitere* – repent) The act of being sorry for one's personal sin* i.e. sorrow for any thought, word or deed which is a contradiction of God's love.

Penitent (Latin – *paenitere* – repent) *Either* one who is sorry for sins* committed, *or* one who is in the habit of using Sacramental Confession*, *or* one who is under discipline as a result of sins committed.

Pericope (Greek – section) A passage from Scripture*, especially one appointed to be read in Church* services*

Petition (Latin – *petere* – to seek) An asking prayer.

Pilgrim/Pilgrimage (Latin – *peregrinus* – stranger) *Either* one who journeys to a sacred place as an act of religious devotion, *or* one who sees life as a journey of faith*. A pilgrimage is the pilgrim's journey.

Prayer (Late Latin – *precare* – to beg for, to ask earnestly) One of the foundation stones of the Christian Life. It is conversation with the Creator*, and built on the belief in the eternal yet personal nature of the God who is revealed* in the Bible* as Lord of history and Creator of the world, and also on the acceptance of the intimate relationship between God and his children shown in the reconciling* work of his Son Jesus Christ. Its primary intention is to seek out what is God's Will for his creatures, knowing that His Will is one of loving care. Prayer may express itself in spoken words, in the reading either silently or out loud of written words (Vocal Prayer) or in a silent lifting of the heart to God whereby the mind aspires to a coming close to him (Mental Prayer). This expresses itself in two forms – meditation (mental prayer using e.g. a biblical* passage to focus the soul's* approach to God) or contemplation (mental prayer which does not need the kind of external aid used in meditation, but is rather the soul simply lifting itself to God in silent love and adoration.) Prayer is an art to be learnt, as our Lord indicated when he instructed his disciples* by giving them the Lord's Prayer.

Preach/preacher (Latin –

praedicere – proclaim) To deliver a sermon* or religious address.

Prebendary 53

Precentor 54

Preface 113

Preface, proper 113

Prefer/Preferment 62

Prelate 62

Presanctified, Mass of the 112

Presbyter 62

Presence, Real 113

Presentation, suspension of 63

Presentment 62

President 113

Prevent (Latin – *praevenire* – to come before) BCP* Communion service – 'Prevent us, O Lord, in all our doings with thy most gracious favour'. An old word which is now commonly replaced by 'Go before' but, in the fullness of its meaning, indicates that God does not so much go before us, but *meets* us with his grace* wherever we may turn.

Pricket 88

Priedieu 88

Priest 49–56, 116

Priest, parish 53

Priesthood 62

Priest-in-charge 40, 41, 54

Primate 54

Principal Holy Days 96–103

Prior 54

Priory 62

Priory church 88

Prison chaplain 51

Procession 113

Processional cross 88

Processional hymn 94

Proctors in Convocation 42, 44

Prolocutor 45

Promulgate, promulge 45

Proper of the Mass 113

Proper preface 113

Property (Latin – *proprius* – belonging to) BCP* Communion service – 'whose property is always to have mercy'. An old word which is now replaced by

'nature', i.e. a quality which is distinctive of God.

Prophet/prophecy (Greek – *prophetes* – one who foretells, spokesman) The Prophets of the Old Testament* were the inspired deliverers of God's message not only about the future but also about the contemporary situation in which they found themselves. They declared God's will to their contemporaries and recalled them to his righteousness. The great prophets all made a contribution to the human race's understanding of the nature of God (see also Section 12).

Propitation (Latin – *propitiare* – to appease an offended person), e.g. Christ is 'the propitiation for our sins' (1 John* 2.1). The general meaning of the word is the appeasing of the anger of a god by prayer or sacrifice when a sin* or offence has been committed. In Christian thought, the death of Christ has usually been regarded as an appeasing sacrifice to the Father for the sins of the world, but, when thinking about the anger of God, it is necessary to remember that the sacrifice which appeases it proceeds, in fact, from the love of that same God.

Prorogation, prorogue 43

Protestant (Latin – *protestari* – to witness before) One who accepts the system of faith* and practice based on the principles of the Reformation*, i.e. the acceptance of the Bible* as the only source of revealed* truth, the doctrine* of justification* by faith* only and the universal priesthood* of all believers. The word originally had a strong anti-Roman Catholic flavour, since it was out of the excesses of that Church that the

Reformation sprang in the 16th century. Protestants tend to stress the transcendence* of God, the effects of the Fall*, and Original Sin*, to minimise the liturgical* aspects of Christianity, to put preaching* and the hearing of the Word* before sacramental* faith and practice and to set a high standard of personal morality.

Proverbs, the Book of 125

Providence (Latin – *providentia* – foresight, *praevidere* – to see before) A quality of God. He foresees the future, not as a spectator, but as ruling all things, and also cares for his creation, providing for its needs and guiding its course.

Province 40

Provost 52, 54

Psalm 94

Psalms, the Book of 125

Psalter 94, 136

Pulpit 78, 88

Pulpit, three-decker 91

Pulpit fall 88

Pulpitum 88

Purificator 113

Purlin 88

Pyx 113

'Q' 130

Quick (Old English – *cwicu* – living) BCP* Apostles' Creed – 'to judge both the quick and the dead'. An old word which means 'living'.

Quicunque Vult (see **Athanasian Creed**)

Quinquagesima 99

Quire 88

Quoin 88

Rafter 88

Rails, altar 77, 78

Reader 57

Real Presence 113

Reception, Office of
The office* in which a confirmed* member of the Roman Catholic Church* is received as a communicant* member of the Church of England* by a bishop* or priest*.

Reconciliation/Reconcile (Latin – *reconciliare* – to make good again, to restore) (see **Atonement**). In Christian thought, the word 'reconciliation' says less about human actions and more about God's actions. God's reconciliation is God's way of providing the means of restoring a right relationship between himself and the human race, made necessary by human sin* or revolt. God achieved this through the sacrifice of his Son – 'God was in Christ, reconciling the world to himself' (2 Corinthians* 5.19).

Rector 54

Rector, lay 54, 57

Rectory 62

Redeemer/Redemption (Latin – *redimere* – to buy back, to pay the ransom, i.e. to ensure the freedom of a slave) The human race is a slave to sin*, suffering and death, and wishes to be rescued from them. The Christian faith* claims that it alone has the full answer – i.e. the Incarnation* and Death of Christ. Jesus expressly associated the role of the servant innocently suffering for his people with the idea of ransom. Christ's ransom effected deliverance from sin and the restoration of the human race and the world to communion* with God (see also **Atonement, Exodus, Salvation, Sin**).

Redundant church 62

Reformation (Latin – *reformare* – to reform) A loose term covering an involved series of changes in Western Christendom* between the fourteenth and seventeenth centuries. These changes emerged from the general discontent throughout Europe with the power of the Papacy (the rule of the Pope from Rome). This became crystallised in Martin Luther's 95 Theses which he is reputed to have fixed to the door of the Schlosskirche in Wittenberg, Germany, in AD 1517, but the impact of which was, in fact, achieved by their distribution to high-ranking theologians, electors and the like throughout the Holy Roman Empire of the German nation. Out of the general discontent, the Protestant* Churches* of Luther and Calvin, and the Zwinglian Movement emerged.

The Reformation in England was a more insular affair. Henry VIII was a convinced traditionalist in both doctrine* and Church government, but accomplished the overthrow of Papal supremacy and the Dissolution of the Monasteries*, being unwilling to have his sovereignty threatened by the power and the demands of the Pope. Although he repressed reforming continental doctrines, he was unable to check the undermining of scholastic theology*. The first English Prayer Book of 1549 (Somerset and Thomas Cranmer), although regarded by some as the thin end of the ultra-Protestant* wedge, presented a faith* and doctrine which was both Catholic* and Reformed (known as the *via media* – Latin: middle way) and, in spite of one or two major crises (e.g. Mary Tudor, died 1558; the Puritan Revolution 1640–1660), the *via media* has been the distinguishing mark of the Church of England* ever since, but the link between Church and State (the Establishment) has also remained (see **The Sovereign**).

Regeneration (Latin – *regenerare* – to give new life to) The spiritual rebirth which Christian Baptism* brings to the soul* of the believer.

Registers 88

Registrar 58

Relics 88

Religion (Latin – *religio* perhaps connected with *religare* – to bind) The human race's response to the trials of the human condition, by which it is driven to seek security, status and permanence by identifying itself with a reality greater, more worthy and more durable than itself. The Christian believes that all religions, even in their most distorted and inhuman forms, are the human race's response, however feeble and unworthy, to the God who has, in his wisdom, so created us that our heart is restless till it rests in him.

Religious order 62

Relinquishment, deed of 59

Reliquary 88

Re-marriage of divorcees 117, 136

Remembrance Sunday 103, 136

Remission (Latin *remittere* – to send away) Forgiveness* of sins*.

Renunciation/Renounce (Latin – *renuntiare* – cancel an announcement) The act of refusing to recognise something any longer – disassociating oneself from something. Christians are called upon at their Baptism* to renounce evil.

Re-order, re-ordering 89

Repentance (Latin – *repaenitere* – to make sorry after some incident) The act of feeling sorrow for one's sins* – a necessary prerequisite (coupled with an intention to try to mould one's life more closely to the pattern of the life of Christ) before

Repose, altar of

Baptism*, Confirmation* and
before Absolution* (see also
Section 10: **Sacramental Con-
fession**)
Repose, altar of 77
**Representation, Church
Rules** 44, 45
Requiem mass 113
Reredos 89
Reservation/reserved 113
Residentiary Canon 55
Responses, Versicles and 94
Resurrection (Latin – *resurrectus* –
risen) The word used to
describe the rising of Christ
from the dead (see Section 8:
Easter).
Retable 89
Retreat (Latin – *retrahere* – retire)
A period of time spent, often in
a retreat house, in silence and
occupied with meditation* and
other religious exercises. In
some cases, the retreat is led by
a retreat conductor. It sees itself
as taking its inspiration from
our Lord's time of reflection
and meditation in the wilderness. (see **Matthew***4.1
Mark*1.12)
Retrochoir 89
Revelation/Reveal (Latin –
revelare – to draw back the veil)
The word 'revelation' is used in
Christian thinking to describe
either the truths about himself
which God reveals to us, above
all in his self-disclosure in
Christ *or* the way in which these
truths are communicated to us
e.g. in the Bible* and through
tradition.
Revelation, Book of the 133
Reverend 50–55, 62
Rib vault 89
Riddel 89
Ring 69
Ringing floor 89
R.I.P. 138
Rite/Ritual (Latin – *ritus* – rite)
The form of a religious service
or services, e.g. the rite of Con-

firmation*, the Anglican* rite.
Ritual has to do with the way in
which *words* are used in a rite, as
opposed to ceremonial*, which
concerns itself with *actions* per-
formed during the rite.
Rochet 69
Rogation days 101
Rogation Sunday 101
Roll, electoral 42, 43, 57
Romans, the Letter to the 131
Rood 89
Rood-loft (sometimes known as the
jube-joo-bay) 89
Rood-screen 89
Roof, wagon 92
Rope 69
Rose window 89
Rubric 114
**Rules, Church
Representation** 44, 45
Rural Dean 55
Rural Deanery 40, 42–44, 46
Ruth, the Book of 123

Sabaoth (Hebrew = 'armies' or
'hosts') BCP* Morning Prayer
– Te Deum, Romans* 9.29,
James* 5.4. Lord God of Sabaoth = Lord God of Hosts (i.e.
the hosts of heaven). This
divine title appears 282 times in
the Old Testament*, most of
them in the writings of the
Prophets*.
Sabbath (Hebrew – *shabbath* – day
of rest) The seventh and last day
of the Jewish week, i.e. Saturday. It was to be kept holy by a
complete abstinence from work
(Exodus* 20.10), a doubling of
the normal daily sacrifices
(Numbers* 28.9) and special
gatherings for worship* (Leviticus* 23.3). The keeping of the
sabbath by the Jews is
accounted for in two ways: the
seventh day represents the rest
God took from his work of Creation (Exodus 20.11, 31.17) or
the remembrance of the
Israelites' deliverance from

30

Egypt (Deuteronomy* 5.15). It was a day for worship, rest and recreation. By the time of our Lord, the sabbath prohibitions had become excessive and were a source of conflict between our Lord and the Pharisees, a Jewish sect noted for the strictness of its attitudes. Since the Resurrection* of our Lord and the Coming of the Holy Spirit* at Pentecost* had taken place on the first day of the week (i.e. Sunday), the early Christian community began to observe Sunday as their day of worship, rest and recreation, a practice which has continued ever since.

Sacrament (Latin – *sacramentum* – originally an oath, especially the soldier's oath of allegiance, but, in the Latin New Testament, the word was used to translate the Greek word *musterion* – something hidden – see **Mystery**) The classic definition of a sacrament is: 'an outward and visible sign of an inward and spiritual grace given to us'. It is a vehicle of God's grace*, the reality of which is made evident to us by the use of understood symbols. The two major sacraments are Baptism* and Holy Communion*; the five lesser sacraments are Confirmation*, Ordination*, Marriage*, Anointing* and Sacramental Confession* (see Section 9: At the Eucharist, and Section 10: Other services)

The table overpage illustrates in simple form the way in which God works through his sacraments.

Sacrament, blessed 79, 107, 114

Sacramental confession 26, 32, 82, 118

Sacrarium 89

Sacred Ministry 62

Sacred Monograms and Symbols 137

Sacrifice (Latin – *sacrificium*) In many religions, the offering of a gift to the god who is worshipped, the gift being frequently a living creature. In Christianity, Christ's Death is seen as the ultimate Sacrifice – a Sacrifice which resulted in the salvation* of the human race. But since Christ made the sacrifice himself, he is seen, especially in the New Testament's* Letter to the Hebrews* (following Old Testament* practice) as both High Priest (the sacrificer) and Victim (the sacrificed).

Sacrilege (Latin – *sacrilegium* – the stealing of sacred things – *sacer* – holy, *legere* – take possession of) Strictly speaking *either* the robbery or desecration of a sacred building *or* an outrage committed against a member of the clergy, but the word is now used more vaguely and widely.

Sacristan/sacrist 114

Sacristy 89

Saddleback 89

St Andrew, Eve of 103

Saint, patron 25

St Paul 130

St Paul's Letters 130

Saints (Latin – *sanctus* – consecrated) *Either* those in the history of the Church* in whom the power of the Spirit* is outstandingly evident and through whom others have become more sure of God and his grace*. They have advanced far along the way of righteousness and achieved a vision of God's holiness (see **Sanctification**). *Or*, following St Paul*, the members of a Christian community (e.g. 2 Corinthians* 1.1 – 'all the saints in the whole of Achaia' 13.13 – 'all the saints send you greetings').

Salvation (Latin – *salvus* – safe) Christian thought maintains that the human race needs

SACRAMENT	SIGNS	GIFTS
Baptism	Water poured. Name of the Trinity* invoked. Sign of the cross* made on the forehead, though this is not essential.	Cleansing from sin*. Membership of God's Family, the Church*. Gift of the Holy Spirit*.
Holy Communion	Bread* Wine*	The Body and Blood of Christ. His indwelling Presence with us.
Confirmation	The Bishop's* hands placed on the head, with prayer*.	The strength of the Holy Spirit (already given in Baptism) to enable the person being confirmed* to undertake the full responsibilities of Church membership.
Ordination	The Bishop's hands placed on the head, with prayer.	The strength of the Holy Spirit (already given in Baptism) to enable the person being ordained* to fulfil the particular responsibilities of ministry*.
Marriage	The joining of hands. The giving and receiving of a ring, though this is not essential.	Union in love*.
Anointing	Oil	(a) Healing of body, mind or soul* (b) Preparation for Baptism* (c) The sign of the gift of the Holy Spirit, indelible in nature, marked on those baptised, confirmed or ordained.
Sacramental Confession	The bishop or priest	God's forgiveness*, and the strength to enable the penitent's* life to be moulded more to the pattern of Christ.

saving from the consequences of its sin*, from the extinction of death, and from the possibility of total separation from God by its own revolt, and that only God can deliver and save it. God achieved this through the Death and Resurrection* of his Son, Jesus Christ, whereby a once-for-all victory was won over the powers of evil and death.

Samuel, First Book of 123

Samuel, Second Book of 123

Sanctification (Latin – *sanctificare* – to make holy) Making or being made holy. Holiness is the distinctive characteristic of God and of all that is specially associated with God. The supreme standard and pattern of holiness is Jesus Christ, God's Son. It is God's will that his people should follow that standard and be made like that pattern. But neither can be achieved without the help of God's grace* which is imparted through the Holy Spirit*. The essential quality of holiness is Christ-like love*. Holiness is a gift from God, but it is also a goal towards which his people can strive.

Sanctifier (Latin – *sanctificare* – to make holy) A title of the Holy Spirit*.

Sanctuary 89

Sanctuary lights 89

Sanctus 96

Sanctus bell 114

Satan (Hebrew – *satan* – enemy, adversary [especially in law-suits]) A title of the Devil*.

Saviour (One who saves) A title of Christ (see also **Atonement, Salvation**)

Saxon architecture 70

Scapular 69

Scarf 69

Schism (Greek – *skhisma* – a split or tear) A word used to denote either a breach in the unity* of the Church*, or the division of the Church into separated hostile organisations.

School chaplain 51

Screen 90

Screen, rood 89

Scripture (Latin – *scriptum* – something written) The Bible* or any extract from it.

Scriptures, Canon of the 6

Season 104

Second Coming (see **Parousia**)

Sector minister 55

Secular (Latin – *saeculum* – generation, age) Concerned with the affairs of this world: usually used as an opposite of 'religious' or 'spiritual'.

Sede vacante 62

Sedilia 78, 90

See 63

Septuagesima 99

Septuagint (Latin – *septuaginta* – seventy) A Greek version of the Old Testament* including the Apocrypha* said to have been made at Alexandria about 272 BC by 72 translators. It is often denoted by the Roman numerals for seventy i.e. LXX

Sequestration/Sequestrator 63

Seraphim (Hebrew) The first of the nine orders of angels* whose particular gift was their burning zeal (see also **Cherubim**).

Sermon 114

Server 114

Service, Divine 118

Services, church 105, 116

Services other than the Eucharist 116

Sexagesima 99

Sexton 58

Shaft 90

Sheer Thursday 100

Shell, baptismal 79

Ship 138

Shrine 90

Shrove Tuesday 99

Sick, Ministry to the 113, 117, 119, 136

Side, north 112

Sidesman/Sideswoman 58
Sign of the Cross 109
Signs, sacred 137
Simony 63
Sin/Sinner (Latin – *sous* – guilty)
The purposeful disobedience of
a creature to the known will of
God – the disobedience from
which Christ came to save the
human race (see also **Original
Sin**).
Slype 90
Soffit 90
Solomon, the Song of 125
Soul (German – *Seele*: Greek – *psy-che*) The personality of the indi-vidual, created by God, and not
destroyed by death.
Sovereign, The 43, 47
Sovereign, Chaplain to the 51
Spandrel 90
Special days 102
Species 114
Spire 90
Spirit, Holy 17, 102
Sponsor (Latin – *spondere* – promise
solemnly) A person who accepts
responsibility for another e.g. at
baptism* or Confirmation*.
Staff, pastoral (see **Crosier**)
Stained glass 90
Stall 91
Standing Committee 46
State Prayers In the B.C.P.* the
prayers* for the sovereign* and
the Royal Family which come
at the end of Morning and
Evening Prayer*. In C.W.*
Sunday Service Book, they are
included in the section 'Prayers
for various occasions'.
Stations of the Cross 91
Staves, churchwardens' 81
Steeple 91
Step, chancel 78, 80
Steward, stewardship (Old Eng-lish – *stiweard* – *stig* – probably
house or hall – *weard* – ward –
one who has care of a house) A
concept, mentioned in both Old
and New Testaments*, whereby
those who believe in God

acknowledge that all things
come from him, that they have
a responsibility to exercise a
proper care of what he has
given, and that there is a need
to respond to his generosity in
whatever way individuals and
communities are best able to
express their gratitude. In the
Church of England*, the word
'stewardship' has often been
mistakenly equated with 'fund-raising'. The definition above
indicates that, in fact, the con-cept is basic to an understanding
of God's purposes in his cre-ation, the place of human
dominion in those purposes,
and the meaning of true sacri-fice, as exemplified in the
sacrificial life and work of
Christ.
Stipend 63
Stole 69
Stoup 91
String course 91
Stucco 91
Sub-deacon 114
Substance (Latin – *substantia*)
(BCP* – Nicene Creed*) The
word used in the Christian doc-trine* of the Trinity* to express
the underlying Being, by which
all Three Persons are one.
Succentor 55
Succour (Latin – *succurrere* – to send
help) An old word which means
'help'.
Suffragan bishop 55
Suffrage (Latin – *suffragium*) A
short intercessory* petition*.
Sunday 101
Sunday, Low 101
⎧ Mothering 99
⎪ Refreshment 99
⎨ Mid-Lent 99
⎩ Laetare 99
⎧ Palm 100
⎨ Yew 100
Passion 99
Remembrance 103, 136
Rogation 101

Thurifer 114

Thursday { Maundy 100
            Green 100
            Sheer 100

Tie beam 79

Timothy, First Letter to 132

Timothy, Second Letter to 132

Tippet 69

Tithe (see Rector)

Title 49, 63

Titus, the Letter to 132

Tomb 91

Tomb, Empty (see Easter)

Towel, lavabo 112

Tower 91

Tower, bell 79

Tracery 91

Transcendence (Latin – *transcendere* – to climb beyond) The word denotes the belief that the Being of God exceeds human powers of grasp (except perhaps that human reason can know that it is, but not what it is). At the same time, Christian thought holds that God is immanent in his Creation. (see **Immanence**)

Transept 91

Transfiguration (Latin – *transfigurare* – to form beyond) The word used to denote the occasion of the appearing of the Lord in glory* during his earthly life (Matthew* 17.1–13, Mark* 9.2–13 Luke* 9.28–36 and alluded to in 2 Peter* 1.16–18.)

Transgression (Latin – *transgressio* – a going over) The breaking of a commandent – a 'going beyond the mark' – a sin*.

Transitory (Latin – *transire* – to go beyond) BCP* Communion service: Prayer for the Church militant. Not permanent. Passing.

Translation 63

Transom 91

Travail (Late Latin – *trepalium* – an instrument of torture) BCP* Communion service: Comfortable Words quoting Matthew* 11.28 – find life difficult.

Trespass (Old French – *trespasser* – to pass over) The breaking of a commandment – an action which is not in accordance with God's Will – a sin*.

Triforium 91

Trinity (Latin and Greek – *tri* – three) The union of three Persons, Father, Son and Holy Spirit, in one Godhead. It may be expressed as God over us (Father), God with us (Son), God in us (Holy Spirit). The Three, being One, are co-equal, consubstantial, co-eternal, but the precise definition of this relationship remains the greatest mystery* of our faith*.

Trinity Sunday 102

Triptych 92

Truss 92

Tuesday, Shrove 99

Tunicle 69

Tympanum 92

Unction, extreme (see Anointing)

Undercroft 92

Unfeignedly (Latin – *fingere* – to invent) BCP* C.W.* Prayer of General Thanksgiving – without pretence, i.e. sincerely.

Unfrock 64

Union of benefice/united benefice 41

Unity (see Ecumenism)

University chaplain 51

Unleavened bread 25, 114

Use – 'Local' modifications of a standard rite* or liturgy* e.g. the Anglican* use, the Orthodox* use or perhaps the use of a particular diocese*.

Vault 92

Vault, barrel 79

Vault, fan 84

Vault, rib 89

Vaulting, lierne 85

Veil 107, 115

Venerable 56

Veni Creator 95

Venite 95

Verger 58
Verger's wand 92
Versicles and responses 94
Very (Latin – *verus* – true) BCP*
Nicene Creed*. An old word
which means 'true'.
Vestments 65, 67, 69
Vestry 57, 92
Viaticum 115
Vicar 56
Vicarage 64
Vicar choral 56
Vicar-general (see Chancellor,
diocesan)
Vigil 115
Virgin Birth of Christ The belief
that Jesus Christ* had no
human father, but was incarnate
from the Holy Spirit* and the
Blessed Virgin Mary. (see
Incarnation)
Visitation/Visitor 59, 62, 64
Visitation, articles of 58, 64
Vocation (Latin – *vocare* – to call) A
conviction that one is called to
pursue a particular profession.
In Christian thought, the word is
used to denote the conviction
held by people that they have
been called by God to a particular kind of work, especially in the
Sacred Ministry*.
Votive (Latin – *votum* – a vow)
Offered in fulfilment of a vow,
especially prayers*, gifts, or the
lighting of a candle.
Vouchsafe (Latin – *vocare* – to call,
salvus – uninjured) BCP* Communion service – Prayer of
Thanksgiving – be pleased to
grant.
Voussoir 92
Vulgate (Latin – *vulgare* – make
public) The Latin version of the
Bible* prepared mainly by
St Jerome in the late 4th. century *or* the official Roman Catholic* Latin text as revised in AD
1592.

Wafer 115
Wafer box 92

Wagon roof 92
Wall plate 92
Wand, verger's 92
Washing of feet (see Maundy
Thursday)
Water 115, 116
Wear, clerical 65
Weathercock 92
Weathervane 92
Wednesday, Ash 99, 103
Week, Easter 101
Week, Holy 100, 136
Wheel window 92
Whit Sunday (Pentecost) 102
Window, Jesse 85
Window, rose 89
Window, wheel 92
Wine 115
Women, churching of 119
Word (Latin – *verbum* – word)
'Word' can be used in two ways
in Christian thought. *Either*
simply the Bible* as containing
the words which describe God's
revelation* of himself to the
human race *or* as a personifi-
cation and title of Christ (see
Logos).
Words, Comfortable 109
Words of Institution 111
World Council of Churches (see
Ecumenism)
Worship = 'Worth ship' The offer-
ing of praise and devotion given
to God.
Worship, Common (C.W.) –
passim

Yahweh (Hebrew) (see Jehovah)
The Hebrew proper name for
God. It was printed as YHWH
and is thought to be connected
with the verb 'to be' (Exodus*
3.14). The name is very ancient
and was certainly in use by
850 BC. From c. 300 BC the Jews
tended to avoid uttering the
name when reading the Scriptures* because of its sacred
nature. They substituted the
word *Adonai*.
Year, Church's 97

37

Year's mind The custom of remembering deceased* persons in prayer* publicly, or by holding a requiem mass*, each year on the anniversary of their deaths.

Yew Sunday (Palm) 100

Zechariah, the Book of the Prophet 129

Zephaniah, the Book of the Prophet 128

Part Two: Compendium

1 Organisation of the Anglican Communion

1 Basic Structure

(a) **Parish** – A subdivision of a county, having its own church and clergy. (see **Incumbent***) N.B. Not all civil and parish boundaries are the same.

(b) **Rural/Area deanery** – a number of adjoining parishes in an area. (see **Rural/Area Dean***)

(c) **Archdeaconry** – a group of adjoining rural/area deaneries. The number of archdeaconries in a diocese is usually small. (see **Archdeacon***)

(d) **Diocese** – an area divided into a number of archdeaconries. There are 43 dioceses in England. (see **Diocesan Bishop***)

(e) **Province** – an area divided into a number of dioceses. There are two provinces in England – Canterbury and York. (see **Archbishop***)

(f) **A Church** – a number of provinces which, taken together, are usually contiguous with the area of a country, e.g. The Church of England.

(g) **A Communion** – a number of self-governing Churches united in fellowship, associated in actions and relations and sharing a mutual intercourse with each other. The Church of England is part of the Anglican (from Latin: *Anglicanus* – English) Communion which also includes other Anglican Churches in the British Isles, and Anglican Churches abroad which owe their origin to the missionary work of the Church of England. The Churches of the Anglican Communion recognise the leadership of the See* of Canterbury.

2 Other words relevant to the structures

Chapel of Ease A chapel* subordinate to a mother church. Where great distances within a parish were involved, a chapel would be established for the 'ease' of the parishioners* to enable them to worship without having to travel to the mother church. Many of these chapels eventually became independent parish churches*, though some still remain. They are normally served by the clergy* of the parish*, but do not have an appointed priest-in-charge*.

Chapter Although the word is used of the clerical* body which governs a cathedral* (see also Chapter House* – Dean* – Residentiary Canon* – Honorary Canon*), it also denotes the body of clergy who serve in a Rural/Area Deanery*. The Rural/Area Dean* is leader of the chapter, and is assisted by a Chapter Clerk*.

Conventional District An area taken from one or more parishes* and administered on an experimental basis as a separate unit. This arrangement is made between the bishop* and the incumbent* or incumbents involved. The district is normally expected to become a parish in due time, and is under the care of a curate*-in-charge.

Daughter Church A church in a parish* other than the parish church*, the responsibility for which is in the hands of the incumbent* of the parish, though this responsibility may be delegated to a priest-in-charge* or other minister*. Many daughter churches have deputy wardens* and their own district church council – part of and responsible to the Parochial Church Council* of the parish.

Group ministry In a group ministry, a contiguous group of parishes* enter into an informal grouping, whilst retaining their independence. The affairs of the group are monitored by a Group Council, whilst not in any way affecting the independence of either the incumbents* or the participating P.C.C.s*. The clergy* of a group meet as a chapter*, with a chosen chairperson. The system of grouping helps to alleviate clergy staffing problems and makes possible interparish co-operation.

Peculiar (Latin – *peculiaris* – of private property) A place exempt from the jurisdiction of the bishop* of the diocese* in which it is situated. It may be a parish*, a group of parishes or a chapel*. Most remaining peculiars are Royal Peculiars (e.g. St George's Chapel, Windsor, and the Collegiate Church of St Peter in Westminster, inaccurately called Westminster Abbey).

Plurality (Latin – *plus, pluris* – more) The holding of two or more benefices* by one incumbent*.

Team ministry In a team ministry the area of a benefice*, which may include one or more parishes*, is placed under the care not of an individual incumbent* but of a team of the clergy*. The leader of the team is appointed by the bishop* and is called the Team Rector*. The Team Rector's colleagues, who are appointed by the bishop and the Team Rector, are called Team Vicars* and have the same status as vicars* with their own benefice and parish. The Team Rector holds the benefice, but the Team Vicars share the cure of souls*. Those in the team may have responsibility for an area or parish or may have some specialised function, e.g. youth, industry, social responsibility. The team meet periodically as a chapter*. The team ministry has a Team Council, the responsibilities of which are the same as those of a Parochial Church Council*, but there may be a number of District Councils* within the team area.

Union of benefice Where pastoral* re-organisation is seen to be necessary and, after consultation, agreed by all interested parties, a union of benefices* can take place. This, in effect, means that one incumbent* has the cure of souls* of two or more parishes*. The united benefice may have one or more Parochial Church Councils*.

2 Government and Representation

1 Elections

To form the various bodies which govern the Church's affairs, two different methods are used.

(a) **Where the clergy* are concerned**, all those who are licensed serve on the P.C.C.* of the parish* in which they serve, and on the Deanery Synod* of the Deanery* in which their parish lies. Clerical* representatives from the Deanery to the Diocesan Synod* are elected by the clergy of the Deanery Synod (the Chapter*) of that Deanery. Clerical representatives from a Diocese to the General Synod* (known as Proctors in Convocation*) are elected by the licensed clergy of that Diocese*.

(b) **Where the laity* are concerned**, the system is different. It is based on a document called the Electoral Roll – a roll of those lay persons qualified to elect to the bodies which govern the Church's affairs, – which is revised every year and rewritten every six years (from 1990). Every parish* has an Electoral Roll. To qualify to be on the Electoral Roll, a parishioner* must:

 (i) Be baptised*

 (ii) Be a member of the Church of England*, or of a Church in communion* with the Church of England

 (iii) Be sixteen years old or upwards on the date of the Annual Parochial Church Meeting*

 (iv) Be resident in the parish, or, if not so resident, have habitually attended public worship* in the parish during a period of six months prior to enrolment

 (v) Have signed the form of application for enrolment

The Annual Parochial Church Meeting must take place between 1 January and 30 April in each year.

Every year at the A.P.C.M.*, the parochial representatives of the laity*, or a proportion of them, of 16 years or upwards, whose names are on the Electoral Roll and who are actual communicant* members of the Church of England, are elected to the Parochial Church Council*.

Every three years at the A.P.C.M., (from 1990), a specified number of parochial representatives of the laity of 18 years or upwards whose names are on the Electoral Roll and who are actual communicant members of the Church of England, are elected to the Deanery Synod* and take office from 1 June.

Every three years, in the year after elections to the Deanery Synod, a postal ballot is held amongst the lay members of the Deanery Synod to elect a specified number of deanery representatives of the laity, of

18 years or upwards, whose names are on an Electoral Roll and who are actual communicant members of the Church of England, to the Diocesan Synod*. They take office on 1 August.

Every five years, (from 1990) a postal ballot is held amongst the lay members of the Deanery Synods to elect a specified number of representatives of the laity of the Diocese, of 18 years or upwards, whose names are on an Electoral Roll and who are actual communicant members of the Church of England, to the General Synod*. They take office from the first meeting of the General Synod after the election. Like Parliament, the end of the five-year term of a General Synod is marked by its prorogation (Latin – *pro-rogare* – ask on behalf of) by the Sovereign* [verb – prorogue].

Members of the General Synod are ex-officio* members of their Diocesan Synod, Deanery Synod and P.C.C. Members of the Diocesan Synod are ex-officio members of their Deanery Synod and P.C.C. Members of the Deanery Synod are ex-officio members of their P.C.C.

2 Representation

A general picture of the structure of government in the Church of England is shown overpage. *Note* Lay persons can stand for election only if their names are on the Electoral Roll.

3 Other words relevant to government and representation

Anglican Consultative Council A Council of bishops*, clergy* and laity*, with its own secretariat, which meets from time to time to monitor and discuss matters of concern to the Anglican Communion*.

Archbishops' Council The purpose of the Council is to co-ordinate, promote, aid and further the work and mission* of the Church of England. It consists of the Archbishops* of Canterbury and York, the Prolocutors* of the Convocations* of Canterbury and York, the Chairman and Vice-Chairman of the House of Laity* of the General Synod*, two bishops* elected by the House of Bishops, two members of the clergy* elected by the House of Clergy, two members of the laity* elected by the House of Laity, a Church Estates Commissioner and up to six members appointed by the Archbishops with the approval of General Synod. The Council's functions include supporting the dioceses* and helping them with their work, helping the Church to develop a clearer sense of direction where opportunities, needs and priorities are concerned, ensuring that policies and strategies are developed to meet those needs and priorities, and overseeing the direction of staff and other resources at national level.

Canon Law (Greek – *kanon* – rule) The life of the Church of England*, in

ANNUAL PAROCHIAL CHURCH MEETING *elects* – – – – – – – –⌐
                                                          ¦
(a) **PAROCHIAL CHURCH COUNCIL**   ¦
                                                          ¦
House of clergy	**House of laity**
Incumbent and other licensed clergy (not elected)	A specified number of representatives ◄ – – – – –⌐
Ex-officio Synod members	Licensed lay workers (ex-officio)
Co-opted members	The churchwardens (ex-officio)
	Ex-officio Synod members
	Readers
	Co-opted members

(b) **DEANERY SYNOD**

House of clergy	**House of laity**
All incumbents and other licensed clergy *elect* – – –⌐	A specified number of parochial ◄┘
(not elected)	representatives *elects* – – – – –
Members of General Synod and Diocesan Synod (ex-officio)	Licensed lay workers
One retired member of the clergy	Ex-officio Synod members
Co-opted members	Co-opted members

(c) **DIOCESAN SYNOD**

House of bishops	**House of clergy**	**House of laity**
The Diocesan Bishop	A specified number of representatives ◄	A specified number of representatives ◄
Suffragan or assistant bishop (not elected)	Ex-officio members – dean or provost, archdeacons, proctors in Convocation, the chancellor (if clerical), the chairman of the Board of Finance (if clerical)	Ex-officio members – the chancellor (if lay) the chairman of the Board of Finance (if lay) members of General Synod
	Up to 5 co-opted members	Up to 5 co-opted members
	The bishop may nominate up to 10 additional members	

(d) **GENERAL SYNOD**

House of bishops	**House of clergy**	**House of laity**
(The Upper House*)	(The Lower House*)	A specified number of representatives ◄
All diocesan bishops (not elected)	The proctors ◄ – –┘	Ex-officio members (if lay)
A number of suffragan or assistant bishops *(elected)*		The Dean of the Arches and Auditor
		The Vicar-General of the Province of Canterbury
		The Vicar-General of the Province York
		The 3 Church Estates Commissioners
		The Chairman of the Central Board of Finance
	*Convocations	Up to 5 co-opted members

its many facets, is governed by canon law, which is contained in a book entitled: *The Canons of the Church of England.* The canons are the distinctive way of regulating the life and discipline of the Church and are binding on the clergy*. They are, of course, additional to the laws of the land, to which every citizen is subject. When a new canon has been passed by the General Synod*, it has to be promulged (promulgated), i.e. made known to the public (Latin – *promulgare* – pro + corruption of vulgare [*vulgus* = the people] – publish to the people). This is done at meetings of the General and Diocesan Synods.* Other Churches of the Anglican Communion,* the Church of Rome and the Orthodox Churches of the East are also governed by canons.

Church Commissioners for England The Church Commissioners were formed in 1948, by the fusion of the Ecclesiastical* Commissioners and Queen Anne's Bounty, to manage the estates and revenues of the Church of England*. Since the Church of England is the established* church of the realm, both Church and State are represented in its membership. The composition of the Commissioners has been revised and consists of the Archbishops* of Canterbury and York, three lay* Church Estates Commissioners, four bishops* elected by the House of Bishops of the General Synod*, two deans* or provosts* elected by all the deans and provosts, three members of the clergy* elected by the House of Clergy, four lay persons elected by the House of Laity*, nine nominated persons – three by the Sovereign*, three by the Archbishops acting jointly, three by the Archbishops jointly after wide consultation and six state office holders, including the Prime Minister as First Lord of the Treasury. The Commissioners are responsible for managing the historic assets of the Church, with the aim of maximising financial support over the long term for the ministry of the Church of England in poorer areas, for support of bishops and cathedrals from whom much of the historic assets came and for financing the past service element of clergy pensions. They are also responsible for certain other functions which may ultimately be transferred to the Archbishops' Council*, including pastoral* re-organisation and determining the future of redundant churches*.

Church Representation Rules The rules which determine the way in which Church* membership and government* are ordered.

Convocation (Latin – *convocare* – call together) The synods* of the Anglican* clergy* of the provinces* of Canterbury or York. The convocations consist of the Upper Houses (bishops* – not elected) and the Lower Houses (clergy* – elected = proctors in convocation*). The Lower Houses elect one of their number as president, who is known as the prolocutor – 'the one who speaks for.' Since the introduction of synodical government the Convocations meet only rarely.

District Church Council In a team ministry*, a district in the parish* having a church* or licensed place of worship* may have a district church council and deputy churchwardens* (elected by the A.P.C.M.* of the parish) who may exercise the functions of the churchwardens and parochial church council* in that district. A team vicar (see **Team ministry**) may be authorised to act as chairman.

Endowments (French – *endouer* – make a gift) The Church of England* and many dioceses* and parishes* have endowments – land, property, money gifted to them over the centuries, the income from which is used to benefit both the clergy* and church buildings.

Ex-officio (Latin – arising from an office) A position held on a synod*, parochial church council* etc. by virtue of one's office, e.g. an archdeacon* is an ex-officio member of the Diocesan Synod* (i.e. not elected), a churchwarden*, having been elected separately to that office, becomes an ex-officio member of the parochial church council*.

Lambeth Conference An assembly of the bishops* of the whole Anglican Communion* which meets once every ten years in England under the presidency of the Archbishop of Canterbury*. The Conference cannot legislate, but the resolutions and opinions emerging from its discussions are passed on to the Churches which go to make up the Anglican Communion.

Order in Council The Sovereign's order on some eccesiastical* administrative matter (e.g. a scheme of pastoral* re-organisation, the closure of a churchyard*) in which the Sovereign acts on the advice of the Privy Council.

Parochial church council A body of lay* persons, elected at the A.P.C.M.*, who, together with the incumbent*, licensed clergy*, the churchwardens*, readers*, ex-officio* synod* members and co-opted members (if any), are responsible for the initiation, conduct and development of the Church's* work both within the parish* and outside, whereby the whole mission* of the Church is promoted. The incumbent and members of the Council are obliged to consult together on matters of general concern and importance in the parish, even though the final decision in any matter may be reserved to the incumbent or higher authority.

Standing Committee The General*, Diocesan* and Deanery* Synods* and Parochial Church Councils* are obliged by the law of the Church to have a Standing Committee, elected or appointed from amongst their members, which has power to transact business but is bound by the directions of its parent body. In a diocese*, the functions of the Standing Committee are combined with those of the Bishop's Council, and it is, therefore, both an executive and an advisory body.

Synod (Greek – *sunodos* – meeting, *sun* – together: *hodos* – way). The system of synodical government was greatly extended in the Church of England* by the Synodical Government Measure of 1969, which took effect in 1970. It was designed to achieve a more effective, 'all-through' and coherent system in which the laity* would play a greater part. Emphasis was placed on the place of the Deanery Synod* in the structure. The house of laity of the Deanery Synod became the electoral college for the election of lay representatives to the houses of laity of the Diocesan* and General* Synods.

The Sovereign The Sovereign has been 'Supreme Governor' of the Church of England* and 'Defender of the Faith' since the time of the Reformation*. The Sovereign appoints bishops*, deans* and other dignitaries of the Church on the advice of the Prime Minister, who, in turn, is advised by other bodies.

The Coronation Service, which is the religious ceremony near the beginning of the Sovereign's reign, falls into three parts:

1. The Sovereign's promises and the acclamation by the people.
2. The consecration* and anointing* of the Sovereign.
3. The vesting, crowning and enthronement* of the Sovereign (and the crowning of the Sovereign's consort), followed by the homage of the people and the Sovereign's Communion*.

3 Ministry

A WORD OF EXPLANATION

Much of the confusion in people's minds about the clergy* and their titles springs from a failure to recognise the distinction between the 'Orders' to which they belong and the jobs they do. There are only three Orders, but a multitude of jobs. This section attempts to clarify the distinction and to give general information to make the titles more easily understood.

1 Orders

In the Church of England* there are three Orders – Bishop*, Priest* and Deacon*. To be ordained*, a person must be baptised* and confirmed*. Candidates must be of good moral character and be both personally convinced and have convinced others that they have a Divine call (or vocation*) to the office. A person cannot be ordained priest before the age of 24, nor consecrated bishop before the age of 30. (Consecration: see also Sections 6 and 9) Ordination is a sacrament* and can only be administered by a bishop, acting as the minister of Christ and successor of the Apostles*. The essence of one Order is not removed by advancement to another Order, e.g. a Bishop remains both Priest and Deacon.

Deacon (Greek – *diakonos* – a servant) The diaconate* in the Church of England* usually lasts for one year after Ordination*

A Deacon *can*:
- (a) Undertake pastoral* duties
- (b) Preach and teach
- (c) Assist in leading the worship* of the people, and officiate at Morning and Evening Prayer*
- (d) Baptise* when required to do so
- (e) Officiate at Funerals*
- (f) Administer the Holy Communion*

A Deacon **cannot**:
- (a) Confirm*
- (b) Ordain*
- (c) Celebrate the Eucharist*
- (d) Solemnise a Marriage*
- (e) Give Absolution*
- (f) Give a Blessing*

Priest (Greek – *presbuteros*) The great majority of the clergy* remain in this Order for the rest of their ministry*

> A Priest *can*:
>> (a) Do all that a Deacon does
>>   and
>> (b) Celebrate the Eucharist*
>> (c) Solemnise a Marriage*
>> (d) Give Absolution*
>> (e) Give a Blessing*
>
> A Priest **cannot**:
>> (a) Confirm*
>> (b) Ordain*

Bishop (Greek – *episkopos* – an overseer) The word 'Bishop' is an Anglo-Saxon corruption of the Latin *episcopus*.

> A Bishop *can*:
>> (a) Do all that a Deacon does
>> (b) Do all that a Priest does
> and
>> (c) Confirm*
>> (d) Ordain*

It is evident, then, that the fullness of ministry* belongs to the Bishop – indeed, all priestly functions are, in origin, episcopal*.

2 Jobs (clergy)

Following ordination* to the diaconate*, there is, almost without exception, only one job deacons* can do. They are ordained to a 'title'* and become curates*. After completing their year as deacons, they usually remain curates for a number of years before moving on to one of the many jobs open to a priest*. A priest can undertake any job (except those reserved to bishops*) although only a relatively small number are invited to occupy senior positions in the hierarchy*. A bishop occupies an episcopal* position but can relinquish that position and undertake any of the jobs open to a priest, still being able to confirm* and ordain*.

In the following list of jobs the Order to which the minister undertaking the job will belong is stated in brackets, but it is necessary to remember that bishops can, as mentioned above, occupy any position. The titles and forms of address given are those which take no account of honorary titles.

Abbot (priest) (from Syriac *Abba* – father: Latin – *abbas*) The head of an abbey* of monks* who is entrusted with the government of that community and is exempt from episcopal* jurisdiction. His insignia of office are the same as those of a bishop* viz. mitre*, crosier* and ring*. The head of a nunnery* is called an abbess.

Archbishop (bishop) The bishop* in charge of a province*. In England there are two Archbishops – the Archbishop of Canterbury and the Archbishop of York.

Title: The Most Reverend and Right Honourable (see Primate)

Form of address: Your Grace.

Archdeacon (priest) A member of the clergy*, usually appointed by the bishop* of a diocese*, after consultation, to whom the bishop delegates a particular administrative authority covering an area known as an archdeaconry*. An Archdeacon must have been in Orders* for at least six years and is responsible for the disciplinary supervision of the clergy in the archdeaconry and for the proper administration of church property. An Archdeacon is usually responsible for the induction* of incumbents* to their benefices* and for the admission of churchwardens* to office.

Title: The Venerable

Form of address: Archdeacon

Assistant bishop (bishop) A bishop* who assists the bishop of the diocese* in carrying out episcopal* functions. Assistant bishops act under the commission* of their diocesan bishops, on their behalf and with their authority. Unlike suffragan bishops*, they have no security of tenure.

Title: The Right Reverend

Form of address: Bishop

Canon Missioner (priest) (Greek – *kanon* – rule) A member of the clergy who is usually a residentiary canon* of a cathedral and has particular responsibilities for education, training and evangelism* within the diocese*.

Title: The Reverend Canon

Form of address: Canon

Chancellor (priest) (Latin – *cancellarius* – a law court usher) In England the title of Chancellor is held by one of the four principal dignitaries of the nine cathedrals which retained their medieval statutes after the Dissolution of the Monasteries*. (The Old Foundation*) The Chancellor is, as a rule, responsible to the Dean* and Chapter* for the Cathedral* library, is closely associated with the government of the Cathedral School and is often assigned wider educational functions. The cathedral Chancellor is not to be confused with the Chancellor of the diocese*.

Chaplain (priest) (Late Latin – *cappellanus* – see Chapel*) Originally a clergyman who was in charge of a chapel. Today the word is applied to members of the clergy who perform specialised duties outside the parish context, e.g.

to a bishop

to a college

to an embassy

to the Forces

to a hospital
to industry and commerce
to a nobleman
to a prison
to a school
to the Sovereign
to a university
Title: The Reverend
Form of address: Mr/Mrs/Miss

Clergy (bishop, priest, deacon) (Old French – *clergie* – root *clerc* (clerk) from Late Latin – *clericus*) (see **Clerk in Holy Orders.**) All persons ordained* for religious service. An individual member of the clergy may be referred to as a 'cleric'. Adjective – 'clerical'

Curate (priest or deacon) (**Medieval Latin** – *curatus* – one having a charge) Originally a clergyman who had the charge or 'cure'* of a parish*, but now commonly used to denote members of the clergy* who assist incumbents* in the performance of their duties. Curates are licensed to perform these duties by the bishop*.
Title: The Reverend
Form of address: Mr/Mrs/Miss

Dean (priest) (Latin – *decanus* from *decem* – ten) Originally the title applied to various officials, e.g. a monk* supervising ten novices*. The dean of a cathedral* ranks after the bishop* in the cathedral at the present time, the dean's powers and duties depend on the individual cathedral's constitution and statutes, but the dean has important functions regarding the various aspects of the cathedral and its life, such as its worship, and retains considerable independence. Under the Cathedrals Measure there are significant changes in the way in which a cathedral is governed. There are three distinct bodies involved. **The Chapter*** is the body responsible for the administration of the cathedral. The dean is the chairperson of the Chapter and, as such, has the duty of governing and directing the life and work of the cathedral on the Chapter's behalf. The Chapter consists of the dean and all the residentiary canons*, together with between two and seven other persons, two thirds of whom are lay* people, and the cathedral administrator (see **Chapter Clerk**) if the constitution so provides. **The Council** is a supervisory body, to which the Chapter is accountable. Its duty is to further and support the work of the cathedral and review and advise on the direction and oversight of that work. It receives and considers the annual budget, accounts and report, and makes changes to the constitution, subject to the consent of the bishop. The Council consists of a lay chairperson appointed by the bishop, the dean, between two and five members of the Chapter chosen by it, two members of the College of Canons (see below) appointed by it, between two and four persons representing the interests of the cathedral community and between five and ten persons having experience of cathedral or wider interests. **The College of Canons** is involved in the formal election process of the diocesan* bishop and receives the cathedral's annual report and accounts. It is also able to raise matters regarding the cathedral. The College of Canons consists of the dean, all residentiary, non-residentiary and lay canons, and all suffragan* and full-time stipendiary assistant bishops* and arch-deacons*. (In the course of the last 150 years, a number of parish* churches have been elevated to cathedral status as new dioceses* have been formed, and a number of new cathedrals have been built. Almost all these cathedrals had a provost*, whose functions were comparable to those of the dean. Under the Cathedrals Measure the title of 'provost' has disappeared and all cathedrals have a dean with the functions set out above.)

Title: The Very Reverend

Form of address: Dean

Diocesan bishop (bishop) The bishop in charge of a diocese* or see*.

There are 43 dioceses in England.

Title: The Right Reverend the Lord Bishop

Form of address: My Lord or Bishop

Examining chaplain See Chaplain*. A member of the clergy appointed by the bishop* to assist, together with the archdeacon*, in examining the fitness for Ordination* of those presenting themselves. An increasing number of bishops have some examining chaplains who are not ordained.

Friar (Latin – *frater* – brother. Old French *frere*) A male member, not necessarily ordained*, of the Franciscan religious order*, established by St Francis of Assisi in A.D. 1209.

Honorary canon (Greek – *kanon* – rule) A member of the clergy who is a member of the chapter* of a cathedral* of the New Foundation* but does not hold a salaried post (see **Residentiary Canon***). The appointment entails certain privileges and responsibilities, including the election of the Crown's nominee to a vacant see*.

Title: The Reverend Canon

Form of address: Canon

Metropolitan (bishop) (Greek – *metros* – mother, *polis* – city) The title of a bishop* who exercises provincial* and not merely diocesan* powers. The metropolitical see* is not always the civil capital, e.g. in England, the two metropolitans are the Archbishops* of Canterbury and York.

Minor canon Members of the clergy* usually chosen for their ability to sing the services in a cathedral*, but who generally have no say in its government. Except for St Paul's Cathedral in London, only cathedrals of the New Foundation* have minor canons.

Title: The Reverend

Form of address: Mr, Mrs, Miss

Monk (Greek – *monakhos* – solitary, from *monos* – alone) A male member of a religious order*, not necessarily ordained*, living in community and under vows.

New Foundation The cathedrals* which had new constitutions imposed on them by Henry VIII after the Dissolution of the Monasteries*.

Non-stipendiary minister (priest or deacon) (Latin – *stipendium* from *stips* – an offering, and *pendere* – to pay) A member of the clergy who assists in a parish* and is licensed to do so by the bishop*, but is not an incumbent*. Frequently a non-stipendiary minister either holds a salaried post in another sphere, or is in receipt of a pension following other employment. Therefore no stipend is received from the Church.
Title: The Reverend
Form of address: Mr/Mrs/Miss

Novice (Latin – *novus* – new) A person received in a religious order on probation and for training before taking the vows of that order.

Nun (Ecclesiastical Latin – *nonna* – feminine of *nonnus* – monk*) A woman living in a nunnery* or convent* under the vows of poverty, chastity and obedience.

Old Foundation The nine cathedrals* which retained their medieval statutes after the Dissolution of the Monasteries* by Henry VIII.

Parish priest (priest) A general term used to denote a member of the clergy who has charge of a parish*.

Perpetual Curate (priest) At the Dissolution of the Monasteries* many of the monastic benefices* appropriated by the Crown passed into the hands of lay rectors* who were obliged to appoint perpetual curates* to execute the spiritual duties of those benefices, under the licence of the bishop*, but without Institution* or Induction*. They were commonly styled 'vicar'*, a title which has become of right since the implementation of the Pastoral Measure 1968.
Title: The Reverend
Form of address: Mr, Mrs, Miss

Postulant (Latin – *postulare* – to demand) A person who is undergoing a preliminary period of testing before being made a novice* in a religious order*.

Prebendary (priest) (Latin – *praebere* – to supply) The holder of a benefice* belonging to a cathedral* of the Old Foundation*, though before the reforms of the 1830s, the canons residentiary* of the cathedrals of the New Foundation* and of collegiate churches* like Westminster were called prebendaries. In cathedrals of the Old Foundation portions of the Psalter* are assigned to each prebendary for daily recitation. In the early Middle Ages the endowments* belonging to a cathedral were divided into separate portions, each for the support of one member of the chapter*. These portions became known as 'prebends' because they supplied their holders with a living. A prebend usually consisted of the revenue from one manor belonging to the cathedral estates, the name of the manor being attached to the prebend. With the transference of the attached incomes to the Ecclesiastical Commission in the nineteenth century, prebends have become honorary appointments in nearly all cases.
Title: The Reverend Prebendary
Form of address: Prebendary

Precentor (priest) (Latin – *prae* – before, *canere* – to sing) In cathedrals*, the priest* responsible for the direction of the choral services. In cathedrals of the Old Foundation*, the Precentor is one of the dignitaries, ranking next after the dean.
Title: The Reverend
Form of address: Mr, Mrs, Miss

Priest-in-charge (priest) *Either* the priest*-in-charge of a daughter church* within a parish*, *or* the priest in charge of a benefice* which has been 'suspended', i.e. a benefice where, for pastoral* or other reasons, the bishop* decides not to institute* an incumbent*.

Primate (bishop) (Latin – *prima sedes* – first seat) The chief bishop* of a state. In England, the Archbishop of Canterbury is Primate of all England, the Archbishop of York is Primate of England. (In the Scottish Episcopal Church, the *presiding* bishop is known as the Primus.)
Title: (in England) The Most Reverend and Right Honourable
(The style 'Right Honourable' does not belong to the Primacy, but to the Primate being almost invariably made a member of the Privy Council.)
Form of address: Your Grace

Prior (Latin – *pri* – before) The superior officer of a religious order* or house. In an abbey* of monks*, he ranks next to the abbot*. A priory* of nuns* is governed by a prioress.

Provost (priest) (Latin – *praepositus* – placed in charge) But see **Dean***. In England the title was used in the newer dioceses* of the head of the cathedral chapter* where the cathedral* was also a parish church* and the provost was therefore also the incumbent* with cure of souls*. The Provost's authority derived from the bishop*.
Title: The Very Reverend
Form of address: Provost

Rector (priest) (Latin – *rector* – ruler) In past centuries the clergy* received tithes (a tenth part of all the produce of lands) as payment for their labours. Tithes were of three sorts:

(a) 'praedial' – of the fruits of the ground.
(b) 'personal' – of the profits of labour, and
(c) 'mixed' – arising partly of the ground and partly of labour.

They were further divided into 'great' and 'small', the 'great' being the tithes of the major crops, and the 'small' of minor produce. When the incumbent* who, in earlier days, did not always reside in the parish*, was entitled to the whole tithes of a parish, he was termed a rector. As appropriator of the tithes (a lay person could also be the appropriator and was known as the lay rector*), he was compelled to provide and endow a clergyman to live in the parish and perform the ecclesiastical* duties. This clergyman was known as the vicar*. The vicar's endowment* usually took the form of a portion of the glebe*, together with the 'small' tithes, because they were usually difficult to collect. If there were both a rector and a vicar living in the parish, the rector normally had the 'great' tithes, and the vicar the 'small'. Legislation during the course of this century in England has led to the abolition of tithes. There is now, therefore, no meaningful distinction between the titles of 'rector' and 'vicar', except in the case of a Team Ministry* where the Team Rector* is the senior member of the clergy in the team and works with one or more Team Vicars*.

Title: The Reverend

Form of address: Mr/Mrs/Miss or Rector

Residentiary Canon (priest) A member of the clergy who is one of the permanent, salaried staff of a cathedral* and a member of its chapter*. In addition to the chapter duties of maintaining the services, fabric and property of the cathedral, many residentiary canons have other added responsibilities, e.g. archdeacon*, director of education, director of training, director of ordinands*. In the Church of England, the residentiary canons (together with the non-residentiary canons) formally elect (or refuse to elect) the Crown's nominee to a vacant see*.

Title: The Reverend Canon (unless e.g. an archdeacon)

Form of address: Canon

Rural Dean/Area Dean (priest) (Latin – *decanus* from *decem* – ten) A member of the clergy appointed by the bishop* to act as a channel of communication with the incumbents*, other clergy and people of a group of parishes* known as a Rural/Area Deanery*. A Rural Dean has no jurisdiction over the incumbents and other clergy of a Rural Deanery. The Rural Dean presides over the Ruri-decanal chapter* i.e. the incumbents, licensed clergy, and licensed parish workers of the Deanery, and is co-Chairperson, with the Deanery Lay Chairperson of the Deanery Synod*. A Rural Dean is known in the Diocese* of London, and now elsewhere, as an Area Dean.

Title: The Reverend

Form of address: Mr/Mrs/Miss

Sector Minister (priest) A term loosely applied to a member of the clergy who is involved in specialised areas of ministry outside the parish* context e.g. community, education, moral welfare, social responsibility, industrial mission.

Title: The Reverend

Form of address: Mr/Mrs/Miss

Succentor (priest) (Latin – *sub* – below *canere* – to sing) The Precentor's* deputy in a cathedral*.

Title: The Reverend

Form of address: Mr/Mrs/Miss

Suffragan Bishop (bishop) (Latin – *suffragari* – to support by vote) The word is used in two senses. Less commonly to denote bishops* in relation to their archbishops* or metropolitans*, by whom they may be summoned to assist at synod* and give their vote. More commonly to denote bishops appointed to help the bishop of a diocese*, under their commission, (i.e. acting on their behalf, and with their authority) but who, unlike an assistant bishop*, have security of tenure. Also known in some dioceses as Area Bishop.

Title: The Right Reverend the Lord Bishop

Form of address: My Lord or Bishop

Surrogate (priest) (Latin – *sub* – below, *rogare* – to ask) A member of the clergy (or other person) appointed by the bishop* or his chancellor* to grant licences* for marriages* without banns*.

Venerable (Latin – *venerabilis* – revered) The proper title of an archdeacon*.

Vicar (priest) (Latin – *vicarius* – deputy) (see **Rector**) Formerly the priest* of a parish* where the tithes* had been appropriated. The distinction between the tithes' status of 'rector'* and 'vicar' having now disappeared, the word simply denotes the priest of a parish.

Title: The Reverend

Form of address: Mr/Mrs/Miss or Vicar

Vicar choral The member of the clergy (or sometimes a lay person) who assists in the singing of the services in a cathedral* of the Old Foundation*. Alternative title – priest vicar – so-called because originally a vicar choral was a canon's* deputy in the performance of divine service*.

3   Jobs (usually laity*)

Chancellor (Latin – *cancellarius* – a law court usher) The law officers of diocesan* bishops* and also usually their Official Principals (i.e. the judges in an ecclesiastical* court, against whose sentence there is no appeal to the bishop) and Vicars-General (i.e. bishops' deputies, representing them in the exercise of their jurisdiction). The Chancellor presides over the Consistory Court*. Since the bishop has the right of sitting with the Official Principal in the court, the court is named 'consistory' because it mirrors the ancient Roman practice of the Emperor administering justice with others (*consistentes*) standing round him. Bishop and Chancellor together form *unum* (one) *consistorium*. Appeals from the Consistory Court go first to the Provincial* Court, and then to the Judicial Committee of the Privy Council.

Apart from presiding over the Consistory Court, the Chancellor's chief functions are to hear applications for and grant faculties* and dispensations, to fix tables of fees for new parishes*, to hear, either alone or with others, complaints against the clergy* for immorality, and to issue, through surrogates*, marriage licences*. A diocesan Chancellor is not to be confused with the Chancellor* of a cathedral*.

Chapter Clerk see pages 40 and 51

Churchwarden At the present time, churchwardens, normally two, are elected annually, not later than 30 April, at a meeting of parishioners,* with the mutual consent of incumbent* and people. The practice of having a 'vicar's warden' and a 'people's warden' is now strongly discouraged, unless incumbent and people fail to agree, in which case the former is nominated by the incumbent, and the latter elected by the people. Churchwardens must be baptised and be actual communicants. They must be at least 21 years of age, and must have their name on the Electoral Roll* of that parish*. Those entitled to vote at the meeting of parishioners at which the churchwardens are elected (sometimes called the 'vestry' because the meeting was held in the vestry* of the church*) are those whose names are on the Electoral Roll of the parish or on the register of local government electors by reason of residence. After being elected, churchwardens, who are the bishop's* officers in the parish, do not assume office until admitted thereto either by the bishop, or, by delegation, by the archdeacon*. The admission usually takes place at the Archdeacon's annual Visitation*, after the church-wardens have subscribed and sworn a declaration that they will faithfully and diligently perform a churchwarden's duties.

The duties of churchwardens are 'to be foremost in representing the laity* and in co-operating with the incumbent*', encouraging the parishioners 'in the practice of true religion*', promoting unity*, and maintaining order and decency in the church and churchyard*. Church-wardens are also responsible for the movable property of the church.'

Dean of the Arches The lay judge in the Court of Arches, (the Consistory* Court of the province* of Canterbury) which formerly met in Bow Church (St Maria de Arcubus) in Cheapside, London. The Court derived its name from the stone arches of the original eleventh century church. Since 1874, the Dean of the Arches has also been president of the corresponding Chancery Court of the province of York. Appeals are allowed from the diocesan* Consistory Courts to the Court of Arches. The Dean of the Arches is the only judge capable of passing sentence to deprive members of the clergy* of their orders*.

Laity/lay (Greek – *laos* – people) Strictly speaking *laos* means the whole people of God, but the word 'laity' is generally used to denote members of the church* who do not belong to the clergy*.

Lay Chaplain (see Chaplain*) Lay* persons appointed to assist, for example, bishops* in particular aspects of their work.

Lay Rector (Latin – *rector* – ruler) A layman who received the rectorial tithes* of a benefice (see **Rector**). By custom today, he enjoys the right to the chief seat in the chancel* of the parish church* for himself and his family, and the freehold* of the whole church, but it gives him no right of possession or of entering it when not open for divine service*. In the past he was responsible for the repair of the chancel, but this responsibility is being phased out gradually.

Parish Clerk (see also **Sexton***) Usually a lay person who assists the priest* chiefly by making the responses of the congregation* in the services and sometimes reads the Epistle*. The clerk also helps in the care of the church. The clerk is appointed by the incumbent* and Parochial Church Council*.

Reader A lay* person licensed to conduct religious services. A Reader may conduct Morning and Evening Prayer* (except the Absolution*), may recite the Litany*, read banns of marriage*, preach, teach, assist the incumbent in pastoral* work, conduct a funeral*, with the agreement of the incumbent and the goodwill of the deceased's* family and administer the Holy Communion*. Readers are formally admitted to their office by a bishop*, from whom they receive a licence.

Registrar (Medieval Latin – *registrare* – to register or record) The legal officer of a diocesan* bishop* who advises the bishop in legal matters, issues legal documentation pertaining to the clergy*, keeps the necessary records, and acts on behalf of the Chancellor* in issuing faculties* and common licences* for marriage.

Sexton (A corruption of Sacristan*) The officer charged with the care of the church*, its vessels, vestments* and churchyard* who often carries out the duties of the parish clerk* and gravedigger and is appointed by the incumbent* and Parochial Church Council*.

Sidesman/Sideswoman (Originally Sideman) A person elected at the Annual Parochial Church Meeting* to assist the churchwardens*. The original function of the sidesman was to ensure the attendance of the parishioners at divine service, but that has been modified to the giving of assistance to the churchwardens in the carrying out of practical tasks at services, e.g. giving out service books and taking the collection*. In the case of disagreement at the Annual Parochial Church Meeting* between the incumbent* and the parishioners, each party can choose half the number of sidesmen/sideswomen.

Verger/Virger (Latin – *virga* – rod) Strictly the official who carries the 'verge', 'virge' or wand before a dignitary, but the word is now commonly used to denote the person who takes care of the interior of a church*. These duties are sometimes combined with those of the sexton*. The verger of a parish church* is appointed by the incumbent* and Parochial Church Council*.

4   Other associated words

Advowson (Latin – *advocare* – to call to) The right of appointing a member of the clergy* to a parish* or other ecclesiastical* benefice*. There are two kinds of advowson – *collative* (see **Collation**) or *presentative* (see **Patron**, but not where the bishop* is patron)

Arch (Greek – *arkhi* – chief) The attachment of the prefix 'arch-' to an appointment denotes that the person concerned is in a chief position, e.g. archbishop*, archdeacon*.

Articles of Visitation Requests for information from, for example, a parish* before a Visitation* is carried out by the bishop* or archdeacon*.

Benefice (Latin – *bene* – well: *ficium* – a doing) A term originally used for a grant of land for life as a reward. In the Church of England* it implied the granting of an office which prescribed certain duties or conditions ('spiritualities'), (see **Institution**) for the due discharge of which it awarded certain revenues ('temporalities') (see **Induction**). There are three kinds of benefice – rectories*, vicarages*, and perpetual curacies*. Beneficed members of the clergy* must keep their Ordination* promises, show proper respect for their office and care for their parishioners*.

Bishopric (see **Bishop** – *ric* = German *Reich* – realm) The office of bishop.

Cession (Latin – *cedere* – go away) The giving up of, for example, a benefice* by a member of the clergy*.

Charge An address delivered by a bishop*, archdeacon* or other person at a Visitation* of the clergy* under their jurisdiction. Charges are also delivered to ordinands* by their bishops immediately before Ordination*.

Clerk in Holy Orders A chiefly legal and formal way of describing a bishop*, priest* or deacon* in the Church of England*. There are lay clerks* who are singers in cathedrals* of the New Foundation* and of collegiate churches* like Westminister, but are not ordained*.

Collation (Latin *cum* – together: *latum* – brought) The institution* to a benefice* of a member of the clergy* when the Ordinary* (usually the bishop* of the diocese*) is the Patron*. This means that the presentation and institution to the benefice are one and the same act.

Consecration (Latin – *sacer* – holy) The setting apart for divine service of a bishop*, or the conferment upon others, by a bishop, of the same office (see also sections 6 and 9).

Convent (Latin – *convenire* – come together) The building occupied by a religious community, usually of women.

Cure (Latin – *cura* – care) A spiritual charge, e.g. cure of souls*. Parish priests* are said to have the cure of souls* in their parish. The word 'curate' is derived from cure, but its meaning has changed (see **Curate**).

Deanery Strictly speaking, the word is used to describe the office of Dean*, but is also used of the house occupied by a Dean (but see also Section 1: **Rural/Area Deanery***)

Deed of Relinquishment (Latin – *relinquere* – to give up) The legal instrument by which members of the clergy* cease to exercise their Orders*. The grace* of the Order, however, is deemed to be indelible.

Diaconate (Greek – *diakonos* – a servant) The first meaning of the word is the state of being a Deacon*, but is also used to denote the period of time a clerk in holy orders* spends in the Order* of Deacon. However, one who is advanced to the Order of Priest* does not cease to be a Deacon, and one who is advanced to the Order of Bishop* does not cease to be a Deacon or a Priest.

Enthronement/Enthronisation (Greek – *thronos* – high seat) The rite* by which newly-consecrated* archbishops* and bishops* are put into possession of their thrones. The bishop's throne or cathedra* was the earliest emblem of that office, so the enthronement marked the moment when bishops were given power to govern the Church* in the diocese* to which they had been called. Similarly, there is a rite of enthronisation at the coronation* of the Sovereign*.

Episcopal (Greek – *episkopos* – overseer) That which pertains to a bishop* (see also **episcopate**).

Episcopate (Greek – *episkopos* – overseer) The word used to denote the period of time a member of the clergy spends in the Order* of Bishop*, or a word used of bishops generally.

Father A widely used title for a male priest*

Freehold Incumbents* hold their benefices* as freeholds i.e. they cannot be deprived of them except for incapacity through ill health, for proved serious misconduct, or for a serious breakdown in the pastoral* relationship between themselves and their parishioners*. Those who have been given benefices since retirement legislation was introduced are no longer able to hold them for life. Lay rectors* enjoy the freehold of the parish church*, but with certain constraints.

Friary (Latin – *frater* – brother. Old French – *frere*) The building occupied by a community of friars*.

Glebe (Latin – *gleba* – soil) The cultivated land from which rents are derived for the maintenance of the incumbent* of a parish*. Every church was originally entitled to a house and glebe, but the house and the land on which it stands are now excluded. In recent years, in the Church of England*, all glebe and glebe rents have been consolidated centrally.

Incumbent (Medieval Latin – *incumbere* – to obtain possession of) The holder of a parochial* charge whether as rector*, vicar* or perpetual curate*.

Induction (Latin – *inducere* – to lead into) The term used to denote the final stage, after nomination and institution* in the appointment of a new incumbent*. Whereas the institution places priests* in possession of the 'spiritualities' of the benefice*, the induction gives them possession of the 'temporalities'. After institution, the bishop* issues a mandate for induction to the archdeacon* or other designated person, who lays the hand of the priest on the key of the church door. The priest then tolls the bell, and is placed by the archdeacon in the accustomed seat of the incumbent in the church.

Inhibition (Latin – *inhibitio*) An episcopal* order suspending incumbents* from the performance of their office when their conduct makes such action advisable.

Installation (Latin – *stallum* – a stall or seat) The formal placing by the Dean* (or a representative) of a canon* or prebendary* in the seat or stall in a cathedral* or collegiate church*, symbolising admission to the chapter*, and the right to perform the duties and enjoy the privileges of the office. Deans are also installed, usually by the senior residentiary canon*. (see also **Induction**)

Institution (Latin – *instituere* – to place into) The term used to denote the admission of a new incumbent* into the 'spiritualities' of a parish (see **Benefice** and **Induction**). The Institution is performed by the bishop* of the diocese* or a commissary (deputy) and, unlike the Induction*, may take place anywhere.

Interregnum (Latin – *inter regnum* – between reign) The period between the resignation or death of the holder of a clerical* office and the taking up of that office by a duly appointed successor (see **Sequestration**).

Letters Dimissory (Latin – *dimittere* – send away) A bishop's* authorisation for an ordination* candidate to be ordained outside that bishop's see* *or* a written confirmation from one bishop to another of the good standing of a member of the clergy* who leaves one diocese* for another.

Letters of Orders A certificate issued to those who have been ordained. (see **Orders**)

Literate (Latin – *litteratus* – able to read) A member of the clergy* who has been admitted to Holy Orders* without a university degree.

Local Covenant A solemn and binding undertaking on the part of churches* in a particular locality, of different denominations*, to do everything together which they need not do apart.

Living Another word for 'benefice'.

Minister (Latin – *minister* – servant) A general word used *either* to denote all those who work in the Sacred Ministry*, *or* more widely still, to denote any person exercising a ministry in whatever sphere.

Monastery (Greek – *monazo* – live alone) The building occupied by a community of monks*.

Nunnery (Ecclesiastical Latin – *nonna*, feminine of *nonnus* – monk) The building occupied by a community of nuns*.

Ordinal (Late Latin – *ordinale* – ordering) The forms of service to be used for the making, ordaining* and consecrating* of bishops*, priests* and deacons*.

Ordinand (Latin – *ordinandus* – put in order) A candidate for Ordination*.

Ordinary (Latin – *ordinarius* – order) A member of the clergy*, usually the bishop* or archdeacon*, exercising the jurisdiction which is permanently and irremovably part of that office. This jurisdiction extends to teaching, governing, adjudicating, and to the administering of the Sacraments*.

Ordination (Latin – *ordinationem* – the setting in order) The sacrament* whereby Holy Orders* are conferred upon a person by a bishop*.

Padre (Latin – *pater* – father) The word was probably first used as a title for a priest* by the Portuguese in their Indian colonies, but is now widely used in Italian and Spanish speaking countries. It is also a name by which chaplains* to the forces are popularly known.

Parochial (Late Latin – *parochialis*) That which pertains to a parish*.

Parson (Latin – *persona* – a person [in the legal sense]) Originally it denoted the holder of a benefice* who had full possession of its rights, i.e. a rector*, but it is now currently used to denote any member of the clergy*.

Parsonage The house in which the parson* lives.

Patron (Latin – *patronus* from *pater* – father) A patron is a person or a body having the right to nominate a member of the clergy to a benefice*. The patron is often the bishop*, but may be the Crown, a cathedral chapter*, a college or institution, a guild, a trust, another incumbent* or a lay person. The patronage of Roman Catholic patrons is exercised either by the University of Oxford or by the University of Cambridge, according to the location of the benefice. In almost all cases there is now consultation between the patron and the bishop, and the bishop and the Parochial Church Council* before a member of the clergy* is instituted*. Under recent legislation, rights of patronage are no longer automatically transferred when the land to which patronage attaches is sold, and there is a religious test on patronage whereby only confirmed* Anglicans* have the right to appoint incumbents. The position of the Parochial Church Council in matters of patronage is also strengthened.

Preferment/Prefer (Latin – *praeferre* – to carry before) Appointment to a living* or other higher office.

Prelate (Latin – *praelatus* – carried before, preferred) A title restricted to bishops* but now not commonly used.

Presbyter (Greek – *presbuteros* – elder) The earliest churches* were administered by a board of 'elders' (cf. **Acts*** 11.30, 14.23, 15.22). At first the presbyters seem to have been identical with the 'overseers' (*episkopoi* – i.e. bishops*) but, from the 2nd century, the title of bishop is normally confined to the president of the council of presbyters, and it was from the president that the presbyters derived their authority by delegation. So the second Order* of priest* emerged. The second Order in the Church of South India has reverted to the title 'presbyter'.

Presentment (Latin – *praesentare*) A formal complaint made by the churchwardens* or parish* representatives to the bishop* or the archdeacon* at a visitation*.

Priesthood (Greek – *presbuteros*) The state of being a priest or the word used to denote the period of time a member of the clergy* spends in the Order* of Priest* (but see **Diaconate**). In the Evangelical tradition, which lays special stress on personal conversion and salvation by faith in the atoning death of Christ, much emphasis is placed on the priesthood of *all* believers – ordained or not.

Priory (Old Latin – *pri* – before) A religious house occupied by a community of monks* or nuns* and governed by a prior* or prioress. It is dependent on the Mother House of the religious Order* concerned.

Rectory Strictly speaking, the word is used of the office of an incumbent* who is a rector* but is also used of the house in which a rector lives.

Redundant Church A church* which, because of its siting or a shift in population, or the need for pastoral* re-organisation, ceases to be viable. A church which is accepted as redundant is then vested in the Redundant Churches' Fund. The Advisory Board for Redundant Churches determines its future and its use.

Religious Order A general term used to describe communities of monks*, nuns*, or friars*.

Reverend (Latin – *reverendus* – worthy of being revered) A term of respect applied to the clergy* since the fifteenth century, and prefixed to their names in correspondence.

Sacred Ministry (Latin – *sacer* – holy, *minister* – servant) A general term used to denote *either* the clergy collectively, *or* the calling in which the clergy serve.

Sede Vacante (Latin = the see* being vacant) The period during which a diocese* is without a bishop*. During such a vacancy, the archbishop* of the province* is normally guardian of the spiritualities (spiritual affairs) of the diocese, the sovereign* has custody of the temporalities (secular affairs). In some dioceses the Dean* and Chapter* of the cathedral* are guardians of the spiritualities (e.g. Durham).

See (Latin – *sedes* – seat) Properly the official seat or throne (*cathedra**) of a bishop*. This seat, which is the earliest symbol of the authority of bishops, always stands in their cathedral* church, which is made so only by their seat being there. The town or place where the Cathedral is located can also be known as the bishop's see.

Sequestration/Sequestrator (Late Latin – *sequestrare* – commit for safe keeping) During an interregnum* in a parish*, the Rural/Area Dean*, the churchwardens* and the Diocesan* Board of Finance normally act as sequestrators. They are authorised by the bishop*. The Rural/Area Dean and churchwardens are responsible for arranging the staffing of Sunday and other services and for collecting the fees which would have been payable to the incumbent* of the parish, or to the benefice* generally. They are also responsible for paying the appropriate fees and/or expenses to those conducting services during the interregnum. A full account of their transactions must be submitted to the diocese at the end of the interregnum. The sequestrators are also responsible for the care and maintenance of the parsonage* house during the vacancy.

Simony (from Simon Magus see **Acts 8.18–24**) It is illegal to buy or sell ecclesiastical* preferment*. To do this is known as simony and is well illustrated by the story of Simon Magus in the Book of the Acts of the Apostles.

Stipend (Latin – *stipendium* from *stips* – an offering, and *pendere* – to pay) The official income of a member of the clergy*.

Surplice Fees (Latin – *superpelliceum* – over a fur garment) The fees which are payable to the incumbent* of a parish* for marriages* and burials* (No fees are payable for baptisms*). The fees belong to the incumbent by right (whoever performs the service) and are taxable as part of the income of the benefice*.

Suspension of Presentation A legal device whereby a bishop*, after due consultation, decides for a variety of reasons not to institute* a member of the clergy* to a benefice*, but to appoint instead a priest-in-charge*. This means that the person appointed has no freehold*. The suspension must be renewed after a period of years no longer than five, unless it is decided, in the interim, to lift the suspension and appoint an incumbent*.

Title (Latin – *titulus* – title) A definite spiritual charge or office (usually as the curate* of a parish*) with a guarantee of maintenance, without appointment to which a bishop* may not normally ordain* people without being prepared to give personal support until preferment* to a living* becomes possible.

Translation (Latin – past participle of *transferre* – carry across) When clerks in holy orders* are consecrated bishops*, their first see* is known as the see of their Consecration*. When they are appointed to another see, they are 'translated' to it and it becomes the see of their Translation.

Unfrock Deprive from priestly* office – in former times persons so deprived had their clerical* garments solemnly removed.

Vicarage Strictly speaking, the word is used of the office of an incumbent* who is a vicar* but is also used of the house in which a vicar lives.

Visitation The periodic visit to inspect the temporal and spiritual affairs of the parishes* within a diocese* or archdeaconry*, carried out by the bishop* or the archdeacon*. Before the visitation, the Visitor can request information by sending Articles of Visitation* to the churchwardens* of the parishes it is intended to visit. Churchwardens are admitted to office at the Archdeacon's Visitation, except in a year when the bishop holds a Visitation. Bishops also have visitorial powers in respect of their cathedral* churches, and usually in respect of religious communities settled in their dioceses.

4 Clerical Wear

Alb (Late Latin – *alba tunica* – white tunic) A white linen garment reaching from the neck to the ankles with tight sleeves and held in at the waist by a girdle*. Worn by the ministers* at the Eucharist*. It is derived from the under-tunic common in the Greek and Roman world, and has been used in Christian worship* from an early date. Because of its colour, it is taken to symbolise purity.

Amice (Latin – *amictus* – garment) A square linen cloth with strings attached worn round the neck by the priest* and other ministers at the Eucharist*. It is put on by placing the amice over the head and tying the strings round the waist. Once the other vestments* have been put on, the amice is pushed back round the neck. It is sometimes taken to symbolise the 'helmet of salvation'.

Apparel An ornamental embroidered strip, usually on the back of the amice*, but also sometimes on the front of the alb*. The apparel can agree with the liturgical colour* of the season* or day.

Biretta (Latin – *birrus* – silk or wool cap) A hard square cap worn by the clergy*. Originally its use was confined to the higher graduates of universities. Its colour is black for priests* and purple for bishops*.

Canterbury cap A soft cloth cap sometimes worn by Church dignitaries.

Cassalb A long white garment worn by the clergy* and others, especially when officiating in church. It combines in itself the functions of the cassock* and the alb* – hence the name.

Cassock A long garment worn by the clergy* and others especially when officiating in church. The cassocks of bishops* are violet or purple, of the clergy, black, and of royal appointments, scarlet. Choirs* wear cassocks of varying colours.

Chasuble The outermost garment worn by bishops* and priests* when celebrating the Eucharist*. It is derived from the *paenula*, the outdoor cloak worn by both sexes in the later Greco-Roman world. In shape it was originally like a tent, with a hole for the head, but gradually it was reduced in size. The chasuble is often richly embroidered and can agree with the liturgical colour* of the season* or day. It is sometimes said to symbolise the seamless cloak of Christ.

Chimère A silk or satin gown without sleeves, worn by Anglican* bishops* and doctors of divinity. It derives perhaps from the tabard, a medieval upper garment. It is frequently worn at services other than the Eucharist* (pronounced 'shim' air').

Cincture Now a broad belt of cloth matching the cassock* (but see **Girdle**).

Cloak A loose, long garment worn by the clergy* over their robes, as a means of protection from the weather.

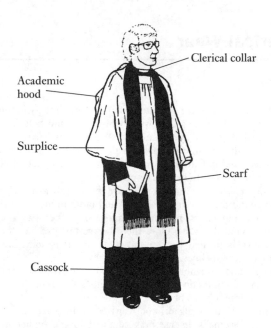

Academic hood

Clerical collar

Surplice

Scarf

Cassock

A member of the clergy in choir habit

College cap A stiffened head-piece, surmounted by a square of 'board' covered with black cloth. The 'board' usually has a tassle fixed at its centre. It is commonly known as a 'mortar board'. It was originally part of medieval academic dress.

Convocation Dress The dress, consisting of rochet* and chimère, worn by bishops* when in Convocation*, on other formal occasions and frequently at non-Eucharistic* services.

Cope A semi-circular cloak worn by the clergy* usually on ceremonial occasions. Like the chasuble*, it derives from the *paenula* or *pluviale* worn in the late Greco-Roman world in cold or inclement weather. The cope, unlike the chasuble, eventually became opened in the front. It is often richly embroidered. The original garment had a hood, but this now survives as a triangular-shaped ornament, attached at the back below the neck-line, which often has a cross or some other sacred symbol* embroidered on it.

Cotta A short surplice* reaching to the waist or a little lower, with less ample sleeves, and a square-cut yoke at the neck.

Crosier The crook-shaped staff carried by bishops*, and sometimes by abbots* and abbesses. It was probably originally no more than a walking-stick, but has become one of the symbols of bishops' pastoral* authority, and is carried by them in procession*, as well as being held by them when giving the Absolution* or the Blessing*.

Dalmatic (Latin – *dalmatica vestis* – robe of Dalmatia) An over-tunic with slit sides, reaching to the knees worn at High Mass* by the Deacon*. It is ornamented with two *clavi* or coloured strips running from front to back over the shoulders. It is often embroidered.

Girdle (Latin – *cingulum* – girdle) Also known as the rope and originally as the cincture. A white rope worn round the waist over the alb*. It is held to be a symbol of priestly chastity and spiritual watchfulness. It can serve to anchor the stole* of priest* or bishop*.

Habit (Latin – *habitus* – order of dress) The distinctive dress of a member of a religious order*. It consists of a tunic*, girdle*, scapular*, hood* or veil, and cloak*.

Hood (German – *Hut* – hat) Although the habit* of a member of a religious order* has a hood which can be drawn up over the head, the word is more commonly used to describe the garment worn by the clergy* on the back which marks the particular academic degree they hold. It still retains the hood shape, but is not put to practical use.

Maniple (Latin – *manipulus* – handful) A strip of silk, two to four inches wide and a little over a yard in length, worn over the left arm by the celebrant*

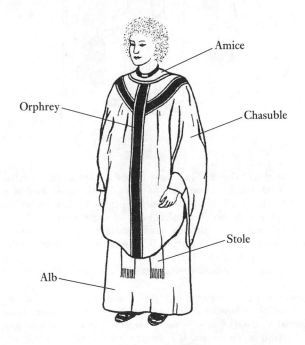

A Priest's Vestments

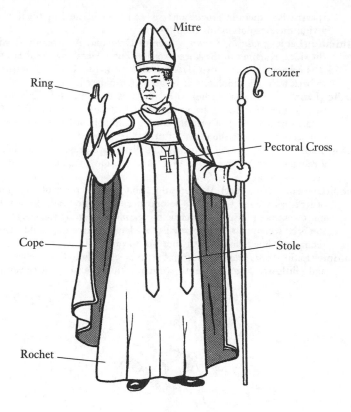

Mitre

Crozier

Ring

Pectoral Cross

Cope

Stole

Rochet

A Bishop

at the Eucharist*. In origin it was a handkerchief carried on the left hand. It is sometimes said to symbolise the towel used by our Lord for the feet-washing at the Last Supper. It is often embroidered and can agree with the liturgical colour* of the season* or day. It is now an optional part of the celebrant's vestments*.

Mitre (Greek – *mitra* – a turban) The head-dress worn by bishops*, and one of the symbols of their authority. It is the shape of an inverted shield, usually of embroidered satin, with two fringed lappets hanging down the back.

Orphrey (Latin – *auriphrygium* – gold embroidery) The ornamental and often richly embroidered strips of material on Eucharistic* vestments*.

Pectoral Cross (Latin – *pectus* – breast) A cross, often of precious metal, worn on the breast. It is suspended by a chain which goes round the neck. Its use is largely confined to bishops*.

Ring (episcopal*) The ring which bishops* wear as a symbol of their marriage to the Church* was first mentioned as being an official part of their insignia as early as the seventh century. It is worn on the third finger of the right hand, is of gold and usually contains an amethyst. In many female religious orders a ring is given at the time when full vows are taken and symbolises a marriage to the Church.

Rochet (German – *Rock* – a coat) The long alb*-like robe worn by a bishop*.

Rope (see **Girdle**)

Scapular (Latin – *scapula* – shoulder) A garment consisting of two strips of cloth hanging over the shoulders down the breast and back which forms part of the monastic habit*. Symbolically it is taken to denote the yoke of Christ.

Scarf A long narrow strip of black material which forms part of the dress of the clergy*. At Morning and Evening Prayer* and on other occasions it is worn with the hood* over the surplice*. At funerals it is generally worn without the hood.

Stole (Greek – *stole* – robe) A long narrow garment, usually embroidered, hanging round the neck and down to the knees, which is worn at the Eucharist*, either by itself or in conjunction with the other Eucharistic vestments*, and also when other sacraments* are being administered. It can agree with the liturgical colour* of the season* or day. When used by a Deacon*, it is worn like a sash over the left shoulder and under the right arm; when worn by a Priest* at the Eucharist with other Eucharistic vestments, it is either crossed at the breast, or hangs straight down as it does when used with cassock* and surplice*; when worn by a Bishop* it hangs straight down. It is said to derive from a neck-cloth or handkerchief. It is a sign of 'orders'* but it is also sometimes said to symbolise immortality.

Surplice (Latin – *superpelliceum* – 'over a fur garment') A garment of white material, of varying length, with wide sleeves. It is a much looser garment than the alb* because it used to be worn over the fur coats necessary in cold climes. It is a standard part of the clergy's* dress when officiating in church or elsewhere, and is also worn by others, e.g. choristers* and servers*.

Tippet Originally a broad black scarf, but now more commonly worn by the clergy* round the shoulders, either over the cassock* or over the surplice* – a shoulder cape.

Tunicle (Latin – *tunicula* – small tunic) The outer Eucharistic* vestment* of the Sub-Deacon*, now generally identical with the dalmatic*. It probably developed out of the ordinary overcoat of the later Roman Empire.

Vestments (Latin – *vestimentum* – clothing) The distinctive dress worn by the clergy* at the Eucharist*, and at other times when officiating at services of the Church.

5 Architecture

A WORD OF EXPLANATION

It is not the purpose of this section to give a detailed account of the various architectural periods, but rather to list the things which are representative of those periods. It must be remembered that the dates given are very approximate, and that there is a substantial degree of over-lap in the styles of succeeding periods. The technical words in this section are defined in Section 6 – hence the lack of asterisks.

Architecture (Greek – *arkhi* – chief: *tekton* – builder) The science of building, or the thing built.

Escomb, Co. Durham, c. 640

1 **Saxon** (Pre-Conquest) A.D. 600–1066
There are very few complete Saxon churches left, but many ancient churches have Saxon work in them. Between A.D. 800 and 1000, very little building was undertaken because of the invasions of the Danes and Vikings.

The distinctive features of Saxon churches are:
(a) smallness – doors and windows are small holes punched in thick walls.
(b) simplicity – a church was a series of rooms joined by narrow doorways. Windows and doors were not decorated.
(c) piece-meal development – extra 'rooms' were added as necessary.

(d) towers – very often of great strength, in spite of being slender in relation to height.

(e) exteriors – rubble walls, sometimes decorated with a criss-cross pattern made of thin stones.

Kilpeck, Herefordshire, c. 1160

2 Norman (Romanesque) 1066–1200

The Normans were prolific church builders and built many cathedrals* and monasteries*, as well as a very large number of parish churches*.

The distinctive features of Norman churches are:

(a) massiveness and roundness, relying on the weight and solidity of the walls to take the sideways thrust of the arches.

(b) method of constructing walls and pillars – two skins of relatively small stones with the space between filled with rubble.

(c) windows, arches and doorways – round-headed and often ornamented. A common pattern was the zig-zag design.

(d) towers – squat and square.

(e) work at high level – in bigger churches and cathedrals, the pillars from ground level supported semi-circular arches to hold the weight of the upper storeys – e.g. the triforium and the clerestory.

(f) roofs – Above ground often of timber and bonded-in to make a tunnel shaped ceiling. Below ground – stone vaulted. Later, the two were married for the external roof – a stone vault surmounted by a steep wooden roof.

Eventually (c. 1160–1200) the Normans began to use a slightly pointed arch for greater strength.

*Terrington, Norfolk,
early English Gothic*

3 **Early English** (beginnings of Gothic style) 1200–1300

'Gothic' was a term of derision given to medieval architecture by the classicists of the eighteenth century, a term which is hardly appropriate in view of the many magnificent buildings of the period.

The distinctive features of Early English churches are:

(a) austerity – a symbol of the emphasis on the theme of the renunciation* of 'the world, the flesh and the devil*'.

(b) height – churches and cathedrals dominated the surrounding countryside.

(c) increasing slenderness, which created an atmosphere of spaciousness – pillars no longer had the Norman massiveness.

(d) pointed arches

(e) longer windows – a number of narrow pointed lancets would be grouped together to form a large window.

(f) use of buttresses – particularly flying buttresses – to take the thrust of the upper storeys.

Patrington, Yorkshire,
fourteenth century

4 Decorated (continuation of Gothic style) 1300–1400
The name of this period derives not from general building styles, but from
the amount of ornamentation and decoration which was introduced.

The distinctive features of Decorated churches are:

(a) increasing elaborateness.
(b) use of decoration wherever possible.
(c) use of tracery in windows, and the increasing use of stained glass.
(d) tall, graceful spires.

Long Melford, Suffolk, late fifteenth century

5 Perpendicular (continuation of Gothic style) 1400–1500

The keynote of Perpendicular design is that of sophisticated restraint, with great attention given to detail and proportion. It is a style which is distinctively English.

The distinctive features of Perpendicular churches are:

(a) lofty slender walls with deeper buttresses and very large windows, with the emphasis throughout on straight vertical lines. The tracery is less elaborate.

(b) lower and flatter arches.

(c) rib and fan vaulting.

After about 1500, the Perpendicular style was modified and is generally known as Tudor Gothic. The Reformation* which followed thirty years later destroyed much that was beautiful, and insisted on simplicity in church interiors.

Not many churches were built between 1550 and 1700.

Ingestre, Staffordshire, 1676

6 Classical Revival 1700–1800

There was a distinction between the styles used for churches of importance (e.g. St Paul's Cathedral in London) and the simpler parish churches.

The important churches were influenced in design by the study of ancient and recent architecture in Italy and France. The classical and baroque (ornate) styles were used.

The simpler churches are usually square or rectangular in shape, often of brick, with round-headed or circular windows. Many of these churches have galleries and contain much fine woodwork.

St Lawrence Jewry, 1671–7

7 Gothic Revival 1800–1900

During the nineteenth century, there was a tremendous increase in the number of churches built as towns and cities grew rapidly in size as a result of the Industrial Revolution. As the name of this period suggests, the architects looked back to the Norman*, Early English*, Decorated* and sometimes to the Perpendicular* styles for their inspiration, but they attempted to interpret them in new and exciting ways, rather than seeking to build mere imitations of the medieval churches. There was a great revival in craftsmanship particularly in stained glass, tiles, woodwork, metalwork and fabrics.

8 Modern architecture 1900+

Experiments continue both in shape and materials.

Twentieth-century re-ordering giving central positions to font, lectern and altar at St Francis, Long Eaton

6 Churches and their Contents

Abacus (Latin *abacus* – board or slate) The top part of a capital*, usually a square or curve-sided slab of stone or marble, which supports the architrave*.

Abbey (Old French *abbaie*) A monastery* consisting of monks* governed by an abbot*, or nuns* under an abbess. Since the Dissolution of the Monasteries*, the word has been used to describe a church which was formerly part of a monastery.

Abutment (Old French *aboutement* – the point at which ends meet each other) Solid masonry, e.g. a wall or pier* which acts as a support against the thrust or sideways pressure of an arch.

Aisle (Latin *ala* – a wing cf. French *aile*) The part of the church on either side of the nave*, usually divided by a row of pillars*. It is therefore incorrect to use this word to describe the gangway leading up the centre of the nave.

Altar (Latin – *altare* – high place) A raised structure of stone or wood consecrated as the place on which the Eucharist* is celebrated. The earliest altars were wooden, being tables in private houses. Stone altars were introduced when it became customary to celebrate the Eucharist on the tombs* of martyrs*.

Altar of repose The altar* to which the Blessed Sacrament* is taken in procession after the Mass* of Maundy Thursday* and reserved for the Mass of the Presanctified* on Good Friday*.

Altar rails The rails marking off the area around or in front of the altar*. They were introduced to prevent the desecration of the altar. Later they came to be used as the place where communicants* knelt to receive Communion*.

Ambo (Latin – *ambo*) The name given to the pulpit* or reading-desk in early Christian churches. Ambos are found in many churches today, usually in pairs, in place of pulpit and lectern*. The Gospel* was read or sung from the ambo.

Ambulatory (Latin – *ambulatorius* – place for walking) Usually a semicircular walking space round the sanctuary* in the apse* of certain churches of the Norman* period.

Apse (Latin – *apsis* – arch or vault) A semi-circular or many-sided area, often with arched or domed* roof, at the east end of the chancel*. Apsidel sanctuaries* were a common feature of ancient basilicas* but only a few Norman* examples remain, e.g. Norwich Cathedral.

Arcade (Latin – *arcus* – bow or arch) A series of arches, either open or closed with masonry, and supported on columns* or piers*.

Archdeacon's certificate The legal requirement before undertaking repairs or maintenance in a church.

1.	East Window	11.	Pulpit
2.	Altar	12.	Hymn board
3.	Cross	13.	Crucifix
4.	Credence table	14.	Banner
5.	Sedilia	15.	Lady chapel
6.	Organ	16.	Lectern
7.	Altar rails	17.	Pews
8.	Chancel	18.	Nave
9.	Choir pews	19.	Font
10.	Chancel step	20.	Memorial brass

Architrave (Latin – *arcus* – arch + *trabs* – beam) The horizontal beam which rests across the abaci* at the top of a series of columns*.

Arris (Latin – *arista* – fish-spine – French 'sharp edge') The vertical sharp edges between the flutes* on a column*.

Ashlar Hewn and squared stones prepared for building.

Aumbry (Latin – *armarium* – closet or chest) A cupboard, locker or closed recess in a wall used for the reservation* of the Blessed Sacrament*, or for keeping the Holy Oils*.

Baldachino (Italian) A canopy either supported on pillars or suspended from the roof above an altar*, throne or shrine*.

Banner Originally the standard of a king or prince which acted as a rallying point in battle. Christians of the 7th century saw the symbolism of this and began to use crosses* with red streamers attached for street processions*. Banners are now common in churches* and are used on special occasions. They depict *either* some sacred symbol* of a general nature *or* one specifically connected with the patron saint* of a church or representations particularly of Christ* and the Blessed Virgin Mary, mother of our Lord.

Baptismal shell A shell, often of mother of pearl and frequently ornamented by a cross*, used to pour the water of baptism* over the head of the person being baptised.

Baptistery (Latin – *baptisare* – to wash, immerse or bathe) That part of a church in which the sacrament* of Baptism* is administered.

Barrel vault A continuous vault*, semi-circular in shape, like a tunnel.

Basilica (Latin – *basilica* – originally a royal palace) The word came, by extension, to mean a large oblong building or hall, with double colonnades* and a semi-circular apse* at the end, which was used as a court of justice or place of assembly. Roman emperors handed over basilicas to be consecrated and used as places of worship*. The word now means a church or cathedral* which has its origins as above, or has been built to the same architectural design. In the Roman Catholic Church, the Pope gives this title to certain churches which he wishes to honour.

Bay (French – *baie* – the basic meaning is 'indentation' or 'recess') A compartment or division in a building, particularly in a cathedral*, where it is marked out by shafts* or pillars*.

Beam, collar A beam in a timber roof which is fixed across the angle formed by a horizontal and a sloping rafter*, to prevent them sagging.

Beam, hammer A short beam projecting from the wall at the foot of a principal rafter* in a timber roof, in place of a tie beam*.

Beam, tie A horizontal or slightly arched beam* which connects (ties together) the bases of a rafter* span in a timber roof, i.e. it crosses the roof space.

Belfry (Originally a movable tower or shed to protect besiegers) *Either* a bell tower, generally attached to a church, but sometimes standing separate *or* the space in the church tower where the bells are hung (see **Ringing floor**).

Bell-tower (see **Belfry**)

Bier (Old English – *baer*) A movable stand on which a coffin is placed before burial*.

Boss A projecting, usually round, ornamented piece of wood or stone, placed at the intersection of the ribs of a roof or ceiling vault*.

Brass A memorial tablet of brass, with figure or inscription, set either in the floor or on the wall of a church. 'Brass-rubbing', i.e. taking an impression of a brass by covering it with paper and rubbing it with, for example, cobbler's wax, is a widespread hobby.

Buttress (French – *bouter* – to push against) A structure of brick or stone built against a wall or building to strengthen or support it.

Buttress, flying A buttress* arched out from a wall to carry roof pressure outwards and downwards.

Campanile (Latin – *campana* – bell) A bell-tower*, usually detached from a church.

Candlesnuffer An instrument for extinguishing lighted candles.

Capital (Latin – *caput/capitellum* – head) The head or top of a column* or pillar*.

Cartouche (French) The ornamentation, by elaborate scrolls, of shields, tablets* or coats of arms.

Catafalque A platform or stage erected to receive a coffin, frequently found in crematoria*.

Cathedra (Latin – *cathedra* – chair) The bishop's* chair or throne, the original position of which was in the centre of the apse*, behind the high altar*, (e.g. Norwich Cathedral). It is now commonly positioned on the south side of the Quire*. The 'throne' is one of the oldest and most important symbols of a bishop's authority.

Cathedral (Latin – *cathedra* – chair) The church which contains the 'throne' or official seat of the bishop* of the diocese* and is therefore the principal church of the diocese, or its 'mother church'. Under the Norman Kings, sees* were transferred from the villages, where they were often originally established, to the chief borough or 'city' of the diocese, and so an identification of 'city' with 'cathedral town' grew up. When Henry VIII created new bishoprics*, the boroughs in which they were established were created 'cities'. The same principle has been applied ever since, with one or two exceptions. Conversely, a number of boroughs without cathedrals have been created 'cities'.

Cemetery (Greek – *koimeterion* – a dormitory, a sleeping place) A place set apart for the burial* of the dead, not necessarily attached to a church*.

Chancel (Latin – *cancellus* – lattice) Originally applied to the part of the Church immediately around the altar*, now known as the sanctuary*, and often enclosed by lattice-work or screen*. It is now taken to include the whole area in the main body of the church east of the nave* and transepts*.

Chancel step The step beneath the chancel* arch, where the Sacrament* of Confirmation* is administered.

Chantry (French – *chanter* – to sing) *Either* an endowment for the maintenance of one or more priests* to sing daily masses* for the souls* of departed benefactors, *or* the chapel*, altar* or part of a church* endowed for the same purpose.

Chantry Chapel (see **Chantry**)

Chapel (Late Latin – *capella* – little cloak or cape) The Frankish Kings preserved the cloak of St Martin of Tours (died A.D. 397) as a sacred relic, which was carried before them into battle. The cloak was kept in a sanctuary in the care of *capellani* or 'chaplains*'. The word was later used to describe any sanctuary* containing relics*, then any private sanctuary or holy place, and finally any building used for worship*, not being a church*.

Chapel Royal A private chapel* attached to a royal court (e.g. Buckingham Palace, Windsor Castle, Sandringham). In England these chapels are not subject to the jurisdiction of the bishop* of the diocese* in which they are situated, but to the Dean* of the Chapels Royal.

Chapter-house (Latin – *capitulum* – chapter, e.g. of a book) A building attached to a cathedral* or monastery* in which meetings of the chapter* are held. The name derives from the custom of monks* gathering together to read a chapter (or passage) from the Bible* or other sacred books.

Chevron (Latin – *capreoli* – two pieces of wood inclined like rafters) Norman* stone moulding in a zig-zag form, e.g. the pillars of Durham Cathedral.

Choir (Latin – *chorus* – company of dancers, or dance) The part of a church occupied by those who sing the services, usually at the east end and often separated from the nave* by a screen*. Alternative spelling: Quire*. This word is often used to denote that part of a cathedral* which, in a parish church*, is called the chancel*. (see also Section 7)

Christmas Crib A representation of the crib or manger in which Jesus was laid at his birth which is placed in a church on Christmas Eve* and remains there until the end of the Epiphany* octave*, 13 January. It contains figures of the Holy Child, Mary and Joseph, the Shepherds, cattle, angels*. Figures of the Wise Men are added on the Feast of the Epiphany* (6 January). St Francis of Assisi is reputed to have made the first crib in 1223.

Church (Greek – *kuriakon* – something belonging to the Lord) A building for public Christian worship*. (see Dictionary section: **Church**)

Churchwardens' staves (Plural of 'staff') Staffs carried by churchwardens* as symbols of their authority.

Churchyard The enclosed piece of ground in which a church stands. The churchyard of most older churches was also the burial* ground for the parish*.

Clerestory The upper part of the nave*, choir*, and transepts* of a cathedral* or large church, lying, if there is one, above the triforium* or, if not, above the arches of the nave. It contains a series of windows clear of the roofs of the aisles* which admit light to the central parts of the building.

Cloister (Latin – *claustrum* – bolt or lock, later a 'shut-up place') A covered walk or arcade* connected with a monastery*, cathedral* or large church, serving as a means of access between the various buildings, and sometimes used as a place of exercise or study. It often runs round a quadrangle, with a plain wall on one side, and a series of windows or a colonnade* on the other.

Collegiate Church (Latin – *collegiatus* – member of a college or corporation) A church which is endowed for a chapter* or college of priests*. Strictly speaking, all our cathedral* churches are collegiate churches in the sense of being staffed by a college of priests, though it would be possible to have a cathedral which was not, in this sense, a collegiate church. Amongst collegiate churches which are not cathedrals are St George's, Windsor, and the Collegiate Church of St Peter in Westminster.

Colonnade (French – *colonne* – column) A series of columns* spread at regular intervals and supporting an entablature*.

Column (French – *colonne* – column) A round pillar* with base, shaft* and capital* supporting the entablature*.

Commissary Court In the diocese* of Canterbury, the consistory court* is known as the commissary court. The judge in a consistory court is styled the Chancellor*, but in Canterbury is known as the Commissary-General.

Confessional (box) The stall or box in a church in which a priest* hears confession*.

Consecration (Latin – *sacer* – holy) The solemn act of setting apart for Divine service* churches, and certain things within them, e.g. altars*, Eucharistic* vessels. (see also Sections 3 and 9)

Consistory Court (Latin – *consistorium* – originally the antechamber of the Imperial palace at Rome where the Emperor administered justice with the *consistentes* standing round him.) The Consistory Court is the bishop's* court for the administration of ecclesiastical* law in the diocese*. One of its major tasks today is to adjudicate, under the direction of the Chancellor* of the diocese, in cases where a faculty* is contested, or has not been sought, when works of an important nature are planned for or carried out in a church.

Corbel (Latin – *corvus* – raven) Originally, when the word was applied to architecture*, it meant the forming of wood or stone in the shape of a raven's beak. It now means a projection of wood or stone, jutting out from a wall (a bracket), which carries the weight of, for example, a beam.

Cornice (French) A horizontal moulded projection, especially the uppermost member of an entablature*.

Corona (Latin – *crown*) *Either* the large flat projecting part of a cornice* which crowns the entablature* *or* a circular chandelier or hanging ornament.

Credence (table) (Latin – *credo* – I trust) (The word became attached to any side table on which meats were placed for tasting or testing.) A small side table, usually placed in the south of the sanctuary* near the altar* to hold the bread*, wine* and water to be used at the Eucharist*.

Crocket (Old French – *crochet*) A projecting ornament on the inclined side of a spire* or pinnacle.

Cross (Latin – *crux* – cross) The instrument of crucifixion*. A kind of gibbet – an upright stake with a transverse bar on which criminals were put to death, being nailed by hands and feet. Jesus Christ suffered death in this way, so the Cross has become the universal symbol of all those who follow him. For that reason, representations of the Cross, in many forms, of wood or metal, are found in churches, particularly on the altar*.

Crossing (Latin – *crux* – cross) The part of a cruciform* church where the transepts* cross the nave*.

Crucifix (Latin – *crux* – cross) A cross* with the figure of Christ fixed to it. Many are found in churches. Small crucifixes are often carried on the person.

Cruciform (Latin – *crux* – cross) In the shape of a cross*. Many medieval and later churches were built in the shape of a cross for obvious symbolic reasons.

Crypt (Latin – *crypta* – vault) An underground chamber or vault* beneath the main floor of a church used as a burial* chamber, or as a chapel* or oratory*.

Curtilage (Medieval Latin – *curtilagium*) The piece of ground attached to a church and recognised as an integral part of it (See **churchyard**)

Cusp (Latin – *cuspis* – point or apex) A projecting point between small arcs in Gothic tracery.

Dome (Italian *duomo* – cathedral, dome, from Latin – *domus* – house) The roof of a cathedral* or church in the form of a rounded vault* (e.g. St Paul's Cathedral in London).

Dorsal (or dossal) (Medieval Latin – *dorsalis* – back) A piece of cloth, often embroidered, which is sometimes hung at the back of an altar* in place of a reredos*, or at the sides of the chancel*.

Dorter (Latin – *dormitorium* – dormitory) A dormitory especially in a monastery* which often gave direct access to the church* for the night office* (e.g. Durham Cathedral).

Drape (French – *drap* – cloth) A cloth, usually of rich texture, which is used to cover the whole of an altar* (as opposed to an altar frontal*) and is shaped to fall in graceful folds.

Easter Garden A representation of Calvary* with its three crosses and a path leading to the Empty Tomb*. It is placed in a church on Easter Eve* and remains to the end of the Easter* octave*.

Effigy (Latin – *effigies* – likeness) A likeness, portrait or image; usually, in churches, a likeness of a deceased person sculptured in stone.

Elevation (Latin – *elevare* – to lift) The vertical plane of a building. (see also Section 9)

Engaged column A column* which is attached to the wall so that only a half to three-quarters of its circumference stands visible.

Entablature (Italian – *intavolare* – board up) The upper part of a classical building supported by columns* or a colonnade*, comprising architrave*, frieze and cornice*.

Ewer (Latin – *aqua* – water) A large pitcher with a wide spout, often in metal, used to carry the water to be used in Baptism* to the font*.

Faculty (Latin – *facilis* – easy) In every diocese* the consecrated buildings and lands and their contents are in the ultimate guardianship of the bishop*. To make additions or alterations to these, a faculty is a necessary legal requirement. A faculty is normally issued by the bishop's Chancellor*, after consultation with the Diocesan Advisory Committee for the Care of Churches.

Faldstool (Latin – *faldistorium* – folding seat or campstool) A movable folding stool or desk at which worshippers can kneel.

Fan vault A type of vault* or arched roof of stone in which the length and curvature of the ribs, which spring from the same point, are similar, thus giving the impression of the ribs of a fan.

Feretory (Latin – *feretrum* – something carried) *Either* a portable or stationary shrine* in which the relics* of saints* were deposited *or* a small room or chapel* attached to a monastery* *or* a church in which relics were deposited, e.g. the remains of St Cuthbert are deposited in the feretory at the east end of Durham Cathedral.

Fillet (Latin – *filum* – thread) A narrow flat band running along a shaft* or moulding.

Finial (Latin – *finalis* – pertaining to an end) The ornament which finishes off the apex of a roof, gable, pinnacle or canopy. The word can also be used to describe the ornamental wood-work which forms the end of an open seat in church.

Flag   Many churches fly a flag on major festivals, saints' days* and days of national importance. The flag used is the red cross of St George on a white background, with the arms of the diocese* placed in the first quarter, i.e. the top quarter nearest the flag pole.

Flèche (French – arrow) A slender spire*.

Flute A channel or furrow in a pillar* resembling the half of a flute split longitudinally.

Font (Latin – *fons* – fountain) The receptacle for the water used in Baptism*.

Frontal The covering, often richly embroidered with sacred motifs*, for the front of an altar*. Frontals are usually changeable to enable them to agree with the liturgical colour* of the season* or day (see **Drape** and **Super-frontal**).

Galilee (Biblical) In medieval cathedrals*, an outer porch* or chapel* to which penitents* are said to have been admitted on Ash Wednesday*, before being brought into church to do their penance*.

Gallery A platform, supported by columns* or brackets, projecting from the interior wall of a church, and providing extra seating for congregation* or choir*.

Gargoyle (Old French – *gargouille* – throat) A projecting spout, with sculptured human or animal shape, often grotesque, used to throw water clear of a wall.

Groin (Anatomical) The edge formed by intersecting vaults* or the fillet* used to cover this edge.

A Gargoyle

Guild Church The church*, often in London, used by a guild as its spiritual base. A guild is a benevolent society which exists for mutual aid amongst its members or for the prosecution of some common purpose. Guilds originated in medieval associations of craftsmen or merchants.

Hassock A cushion for kneeling.

Hatchment (a contraction of the word 'achievement') A large, usually diamond-shaped, tablet of stone, marble or wood, depicting the armorial bearings of a deceased* person, often found in churches*.

High altar The main altar* of a church, standing in the centre of the east end. (see **Altar**)

Holy table An altar*.

Icon (Greek – *eikon* – image) A flat picture, usually painted in egg tempera on wood, but also carved in mosaic, ivory or other materials. It represents the Lord, the Blessed Virgin Mary or other saints* and is used and venerated principally in the Eastern Orthodox Churches.

Jesse window A church* window based in design on the descent of Christ* from the royal line of the Old Testament's* King David. In most cases, it pictures a tree springing from and beginning with Jesse, the father of David, and ending with Jesus or the Blessed Virgin Mary with the Holy Child. Examples can be seen in Wells Cathedral*, Dorchester Abbey* near Oxford and St George's, Hanover Square, London.

King post A vertical post from the centre of the tie-beam* to the rafter* top. Queen posts serve the same purpose, but stand in pairs.

Lady chapel A chapel* dedicated to the Blessed Virgin Mary, when it forms part of a larger church.

Lancet (Latin – *lancea* – weapon with shaft and pointed metal head) A slender window with pointed head.

Lantern (Latin – *lanterna* – light) A round or many-sided structure, with windows to admit light, often surmounting a tower* or dome* e.g. Ely Cathedral.

Lectern (Latin – *legere* – to read [past participle – *lectum*]) A reading or singing desk in church, but especially the desk on which the Bible* stands. Normally in wood or metal, and often ornately carved or moulded.

Lent array Altar* frontals* and vestments* used during the season* of Lent* and usually made from unbleached linen.

Lierne vaulting (French – *clematis*) The purely decorative short-rib vaulting characteristic of Perpendicular architecture*, whereby the short ribs connect the bosses* and intersections of the principal ribs*.

Light (German – *Licht*, Latin *lux* – light) The perpendicular division of a mullioned* window.

Lintel (Old French – *lintel* – threshold) A horizontal beam or stone slab above a door or window, supported at either end by column* or walls, which takes the weight of the masonry above to allow for the cavity of the opening.

Lozenge (Old French – *losenge* – tombstone) A diamond-shaped shield on which the arms of a spinster or widow are emblazoned. Often found in churches or chapels* which have connections with noble families.

Lych-gate (German – *Leiche* – corpse) The roofed gateway of a churchyard* where the coffin awaits the arrival of the minister* who is to conduct the funeral*.

Memorial (Latin – *memorialis* – mindful of) A sculpture, tablet* or plate erected in a church in memory of a person or persons who had connections with that church.

Mensa (Latin – table) The flat stone which forms the top of an altar*

Minster (Old English – *mynster*. Latin – *monasterium* – monastery*) *Either*, originally, any monastic establishment or its church *or* a large or important church, e.g. cathedrals* – York, Southwell, Lincoln: churches – Beverley, Wimborne. The word is used of those churches from which, in Saxon times, before the proliferation of parish churches*, priests* went out to evangelise (see **evangelism**) the surrounding area. Some place-names include the word, e.g. Minster Lovell, which usually implies the place was the site of a house of secular* canons*.

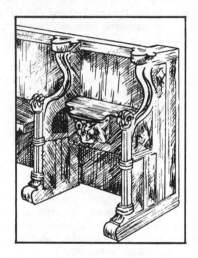

A Misericord

Misericord (Latin – *misericordia* – 'pity' + 'heart' – a compassionate heart) The projection on the hinged underside of a choir-stall*, often richly and sometimes humorously carved, which was probably designed to give support to those who found it difficult to stand for long periods during Divine worship*.

Monument (Latin – *monere* – to remind) A stone or other structure placed over a grave* or in a church to commemorate a dead person.

Mullion A vertical bar dividing the lights* of a window.

Narthex (Greek – *narthex* – a small case) In early Christian churches, particularly Byzantine, the area at the west end of the nave*, from which it was separated by columns*, wall or rails. It was used by catechumens*, candidates for baptism*, penitents* and women.

Nave (Latin – *navis* – a ship) The body of a church, excluding chancel*, choir*, baptistery* and aisles*, which is assigned to the laity*. A ship was often used as a symbol of the church (cf. the symbol of the World Council of Churches – see Dictionary section: **Ecumenism** and Section 14)

Nave altar (see **altar**) The altar which stands at the head of the nave*. Nave altars have become increasingly common in recent years and help to underline the partnership of worship* between clergy* and laity* by breaking down the barriers of distance and separation.

Oratory (Latin – *oratorium* – place of prayer) A small chapel* or place for private worship* not necessarily in a church.

Organ (Greek – *organon* – tool) The musical instrument of pipes, supplied with wind by bellows, sounded by keys and distributed into ranks of stops having a special tone which, in turn, form groups or partial groups (e.g. great, choir, swell, solo, pedal) with separate key boards, which is normally used to provide music in churches *. The instrument is played by an organist.

Pall (Latin – *pallium* – cloak) A cloth, usually of black, purple or white material, spread over a coffin*. (see also **Pall: Section 9**)

Parclose (Old French – *parclos* – closed off) A screen* or set of railings, usually at the east end of an aisle*, to enclose a chantry* altar* for requiem masses*.

Parish church (see **parish** and **church**) In England, the church serving an area under the spiritual care of a member of the Church of England's* clergy to whose religious ministrations all its inhabitants are entitled.

Parvis (Old French – *pare(v)is*. Latin – *paradisus* – paradise) Originally the court in front of a cathedral* or large church. Later, the portico* (roofed colonnade*) of a church porch*.

Paschal Candle (Hebrew – *pesakh* – Passover) The candle placed on a large separate candlestick on the north side of the sanctuary*, the lighting of which takes place during the Easter* Vigil* on Easter Eve*. The candle is marked with the sign of the Cross*, the Alpha and Omega symbols*, the year, and five studs (large grains of incense*, gilded) are inserted representing the wounds of Christ. It burns during all principal services from Easter* to Pentecost*.

Peal *Either* a set of bells, usually 6, 8 or 10, hung in the belfry* of a church *or* the sound made by ringing a set of bells, usually in a series of 'changes' which achieve a changing pattern of sound.

Pew (derived from Latin – *podium* – pedestal or raised seat) A fixed wooden bench providing seating for the congregation*. Before A.D. 1300 it was not customary to have seating in the body of the church, though stone seats were built along the walls for the infirm.

Pier *Either* a solid mass of masonry between windows *or* a pillar* *or* the masonry from which an arch springs.

Pillar (Late Latin – *pila* – pillar) A free-standing vertical structure of stone or wood, slender in proportion relative to its height, which acts as a support, e.g. of an arch. It is often decorated or ornamented.

Piscina (derived from Latin – *piscis* – fish. Originally an ancient Roman bathing pond, or fish-pond.) A niche or basin set in the wall of the sanctuary* on the south side of the altar*, used to carry away the water with which the priest's* hands are washed at the Eucharist* (see **lavabo**), and to dispose of the water with which the chalice* and paten* are washed after the Eucharist (see **ablutions**). It has a drain which goes to earth called a sacrarium (Latin – *sacer* – holy). The word 'sacrarium' can also be used as an alternative for 'sanctuary*'.

Plinth (Greek – *plinthos* – tile or brick) *Either* the lower projecting square base of a column* or pillar* *or* the projecting part of a wall immediately above ground.

Porch (Latin – *porticus* – porch) The covered approach to the entrance of a church.

Portico (Latin – *porticus* – porch, from *porta* – door) A roof supported by columns* at regular intervals attached as a porch* to a church.

Pricket (derived from a buck in second year with straight unbranched horns) A stand containing one or more upright spikes on which to fix votive* candles.

Prie-Dieu (French – pray God) A kneeling desk.

Priory church (Latin – *prior* – superior, chief officer) A church which was formerly the church of a religious order* presided over by a prior* or prioress.

Processional Cross (see **Cross**) A cross mounted on a pole and carried at the head of a procession* in church.

Pulpit (Latin – *pulpitum* – platform) An elevated stand of stone or wood for the preacher* or reader. In early Christian times, the bishop* preached from his cathedra*. Later the ambo* was used for the sermon*. Pulpits came into general use in the later Middle Ages.

Pulpit Fall The piece of cloth, often embroidered or with sacred symbols*, which hangs from the pulpit* desk.

Pulpitum (Latin – *pulpitum* – platform) The stone screen* which separates the choir* from the nave* in a cathedral* or large church.

Purlin A horizontal beam, one, two, or more, running along the length of a roof to support the rafters* or roof boards.

Quire (see **Choir** in this section, but also in Section 7)

Quoin (French – *coin* – corner) The external angle of a building, or the stones or bricks forming that angle.

Rafter A sloping beam which forms part of the framework on which the roof-covering is held.

Registers (Late Latin – *regesta* – things recorded) The books in which details of services, baptisms*, confirmations*, marriages* and burials* are kept for reference.

Relics (see **Reliquary**) Part of a saint's* body or belongings kept after death as an object of reverence.

Reliquary A receptacle for relics* – the remains of a saint*, or of sacred objects which have been in contact with the saint's body. One of the most famous examples is the shrine* of the Three Kings (see **Epiphany**) in Cologne Cathedral in Germany.

Re-order, re-ordering Improvements carried out in a church*. Very often they are made to improve the way in which the liturgy* is performed. For example, the establishment of an altar* area at the head of the nave* of a church will a) improve the congregation's* ability to see what is going on, b) bring the action closer to the congregation, thus helping to emphasise the partnership of clergy* and congregation in worship* and c) allow a greater freedom of movement for the participating ministers*. But re-ordering can also involve developing unused space in a church for specific purposes e.g. a meeting room, a parish* office.

Reredos (*Rere* = rear. French – *dos* – back) Any decorated screen* in wood, stone or alabaster which is erected above and behind an altar*. (see **Triptych**)

Retable (Latin – *retabulum* – from *retrotabulum* – rear table) A frame enclosing decorated panels placed above the back of an altar (see also **Reredos**)

Retrochoir (Latin – *retro* – backwards) The part of a cathedral* or large church behind the high altar*.

Rib vault A vault* which has ribs in wood or stone projecting along its groins*.

Riddell (French – *rideau* – curtain) Curtains hung between riddell-posts at the sides and back of an altar*.

Ringing floor The place or room in a belfry* where the bell-ringers stand to peal* the bells.

Rood (Old English – *rod* – cross) A cross* or crucifix*, generally with figures of the Blessed Virgin Mary and St John, the Beloved Disciple, usually raised on or above a rood-screen*.

Rood-loft The means of access for cleaning, lighting or decorating the rood*, and sometimes acting as a base for it. It was also used to provide accommodation for choir* and instrumentalists.

Rood-screen The screen of wood or stone below the rood* separating the chancel* from the nave*.

Rose window (see **Wheel-window**)

Sacrarium (Latin – *sacer* – holy) The sanctuary* of a church*. The word has its source in the Roman custom of setting a room in a house apart as a shrine* for the household gods.

Sacristy (Latin – *sacer* – holy) A room in a church* or chapel* for keeping the sacred vessels and for the vesting (see **Vestments**) of the clergy*.

Saddle-back A tower roof with two opposite gables.

Sanctuary (Latin – *sacer* – holy) The part of a church which contains the principal altar*.

Sanctuary lights Lights hung in the sanctuary* of a church*. A red light indicates a call to prayer*, a white light indicates that the Blessed Sacrament* is reserved* and a blue light is customarily hung in a lady chapel*

A Rood-screen

Screen A partition of wood, stone or metal dividing one part of a church from another, particularly the choir* from the nave*.

Sedilia (Latin – *sedile* – seat) The seats for the celebrant*, deacon*, and sub-deacon* at the Eucharist*, on the south side of the chancel*. Often in the form of stone benches, but also in wood, sometimes with richly carved canopies.

Shaft The part of a column* between the capital* and the base.

Shrine (Latin – *scrinium* – chest) In its original sense the word was applied to a chest or box holding the relics* of saints*. It is now commonly used either of sacred images kept in a church or of any holy place, especially now connected with pilgrimages* (e.g. Walsingham).

Slype (variation of 'slip') A passage from a cathedral* transept* to a chapter-house* or deanery*. (see Section 3)

Soffit (Latin – *suffixus* – fastened) The under-surface of an architrave*, arch or balcony.

Spandrel *Either* the triangular wall surface in the angle between two arches *or* between an arch and the surrounding rectangular moulding or framework.

Spire A tapering structure in the form of a tall cone or pyramid rising above the tower* of a church*.

Stained-glass Transparent coloured glass used in church windows to produce a picture or design. The colouring is achieved not by painting but by impregnation.

Stall A fixed seat for clergy* or others on both sides of the choir* of a cathedral* or other large church. Stalls are often separated by projecting arms, frequently richly carved, and sometimes surmounted by canopies. If the seat is hinged, it is called a misericord*.

Stations of the Cross (Latin – *stare* – to stand) A series of fourteen pictures or carvings depicting incidents in the last journey of Jesus Christ – from Pontius Pilate's house to the placing of Christ in the tomb. They are used for devotional purposes, especially in Lent* and Passiontide*, and are commonly arranged round the walls of a church. Prayers and a short meditation (see **Prayer**) on each incident are spoken in front of each station. The custom is derived from the ancient practice of pilgrims* in Jerusalem following the route from Pilate's house to Calvary*.

Steeple A tower surmounted by a spire* rising above the roof of a church.

Stoup A basin near the entrance of a church containing holy water with which the faithful may sprinkle themselves.

String course The projecting horizontal band or moulding on the surface of a wall.

Stucco (German – *Stuck* – piece) Kinds of plaster or cement used for coating wall surfaces and often moulded to form decorations.

Superfrontal (Latin – *super* – over) A covering which hangs over the upper edge of an altar* frontal*.

Tablet A small stone slab, usually placed on the wall of a church, with an inscription commemorating a dead person or persons.

Terrier and Inventory (Latin – *terrarius liber* – book of lands – *inventorium* – detailed list) The detailed list of lands, goods and ornaments belonging to a parish church*. Churchwardens* are also required to keep a log-book listing repairs, changes or additions to the fabric and goods.

Tester (French – *tête* – head) (see **baldachino**)

Three-decker pulpit (see **pulpit**) A three-storeyed construction, with the parish-clerk's's* stall at the bottom, the incumbent's* stall in the middle, and the pulpit* (or preaching desk) at the top.

Tomb (Greek – *tumbos* – sepulchral mound) *Either* a hole made in the ground or rock to receive a dead body *or* a vault*, often underground, for the dead *or* a monument* to a dead person.

Tower (Latin – *turris* – tower) A tall, usually square, structure forming part of a church. Many churches have one or more towers at their west end. Many cathedrals* and large churches have a tower above the crossing*.

Tracery The ornamental stonework in the head of a window.

Transept (Latin – *trans* – across: *septum* – enclosure) The arms of a cruciform* church set at right angles to the nave* and choir*, usually aligned north and south.

Transom (Latin – *trans* – across) A horizontal bar of wood or stone across a window, or the top of a door.

Triforium (Latin – *fores* – door) The first-floor stage of a medieval cathedral* or church lying between the nave*, arcade*, and the clerestory*. It is usually arcaded*.

Triptych (Greek – *tri* – three, *ptusso* – fold) A picture or carving on three panels, side by side, and often hinged to allow closure. A triptych is often placed behind an altar* to form a reredos*.

Truss A supporting beam.

Tympanum (Greek – *tumpanon* – drum) A large semi-circular stone often used in Norman* churches to support the wall above a door opening or window.

Undercroft (see **crypt**)

Vault (Latin – *volvere* – to roll) An arched covering in brick, stone or wood.

Verger's wand (Latin – *virga* – rod) A rod, often with decorated head, carried by vergers* as a symbol of their authority.

Vestry (Latin – *vestiarium* – wardrobe) The room attached to a church in which vestments* are kept, and in which the clergy* or choir* robe.

Voussoir (Latin – *volvere* – to roll) Each of the wedge-shaped or tapered stones forming an arch.

Wafer box A box, of wood or metal, which contains the wafers* to be used at the Eucharist*.

Wagon roof A barrel-vaulted* wooden roof i.e. it refers to its similarity to a covered wagon.

Wall plate The horizontal timber which extends lengthwise along the top of a wall immediately under a timber roof.

Weathercock A revolving pointer, often in the shape of a cockerel, mounted on church spires* to show the wind direction.

Weathervane (see **Weathercock**)

Wheel-window A circular window with tracery* radiating from the centre. Also known as a rose-window.

7 Music

1 General words

Anthem (Greek – *antiphona* – things sounding in response) Originally a piece of church music sung antiphonally, i.e. lines sung alternately by different parts of the choir*. It is now a general term to denote any piece of special music sung by the choir during divine service*.

Antiphon (Greek – *antiphonon* – something sung alternately by two choirs*) A sentence of Scripture* e.g. the verse of a psalm*, sung or recited usually responsively by a choir.

Cantata (Latin – *cantare* – to sing) A piece of music consisting of a series of recitatives and arias for solo voices, concluding with a chorale (a single hymn or tune) sung in parts by a choir*. (see **Oratorio**)

Canticle (Latin – *canticum* – song) A little song or hymn. The setting to music of certain passages from the Old and New Testaments*. (see sub-section 2 of this Section)

Cantor (Latin – *cantare* – to sing) A singer who leads in the intoning of the music of, e.g. Morning and Evening Prayer*, or of a procession*.

Cantoris (Latin – *cantare* – to sing) The place of the cantor*, traditionally though not always on the north side of the choir* of a cathedral* or church. The word is also used to describe the members of the choir* sitting on the same side as the cantor. (See **Decani**)

Carol (Greek – *khoraules* – flute player) A joyful song, usually connected with Christmas* or Easter* but also with other seasons* of the Church's Year*. It seems originally to have been connected with dancing. Carols are the folk-songs of Church music.

Choir (Greek – *khoros* – song and dance) A band of singers performing or leading in the musical parts of a church service.

Choir office Those of the daily offices* sung by the choir* i.e. Morning and Evening Prayer*

Chorister (Medieval Latin – *chorista*) A member of a choir*, especially a choir-boy or girl.

Decani (Latin – *decem* – ten) That part of the choir* which sits in a cathedral* on the same side of the Choir* as the Dean*, traditionally the south side. (see **Cantoris**)

Doxology (Greek – *doxologia* – words of glory) A giving of glory to the Blessed Trinity* e.g. at the end of the singing or recitation of psalms* – 'Glory be to the Father, and to the Son and to the Holy Spirit'. Several hymns* have a doxology as their last verse.

Gradual hymn (Latin – *gradus* – step) The hymn sung between the Epistle* and Gospel* at the Eucharist*. (see **Gradual**)

Intone (Latin – *intonare*) To recite in a singing voice.

Introit hymn (Latin – *introire* – go in) A hymn sung as the priest* approaches the altar* to celebrate the Eucharist*.

Lay Clerk An adult male member of a cathedral* choir*.

Motet A piece of music consisting of polyphonic chanting, usually unaccompanied. Thomas Tallis, William Byrd and Henry Purcell are amongst the best-known English composers of motets.

Offertory hymn (Ecclesiastical Latin – *offertorium* – offering) A hymn sung whilst the elements* are being placed on the altar*, and the collection* taken at the Eucharist*.

Office hymn (Latin – *officium* – service) A hymn sung in the course of a daily office*, and, properly, connected with the theme of the office.

Oratorio (The name given to musical services sung at the oratory* of St Philip Neri in Italy) A semi-dramatic musical composition, usually on a sacred theme, performed by soloists, chorus and orchestra, without action, scenery or costume. The best known oratorio is Handel's 'Messiah'. (see **Cantata**)

Plainsong Traditional church* music in medieval modes and free rhythm, sung in unison.

Precentor (Latin – *prae* – before, *canere* to sing) In cathedrals*, the priest* responsible for the direction of the choral (sung) services.

Processional hymn A hymn sung in procession*, often at the beginning of a service, and usually on a festival, as the clergy* and choir* enter the church.

Psalm (Greek – *psalmos* – song) A sacred song from the Book of Psalms* (the Psalter) in the Old Testament*.

Psalter (Greek – *psalterion* – an instrument played by twanging) The book of Psalms*, but also the same book set for liturgical* use.

Quire An alternative word for 'Choir'*, but more often used in an architectural sense. (see Section 6)

Succentor (Latin – *sub* – below, *canere* to sing) The precentor's* deputy in a cathedral*.

Versicles and Responses (Latin – *versiculus* – short verse, *responsum* – response, reply) A versicle is a short verse, often taken from a psalm* which is said, or sung by a cantor*, in Morning and Evening Prayer*. It is answered by a response from the congregation*.

2 Prayer Book Canticles

Benedicite (Latin – Bless ye) The canticle* which begins 'O all ye Works of the Lord, bless ye the Lord'. (Morning Prayer*) C.W.*, 'Bless the Lord all you works of the Lord.' Song of the Three Holy Children verses 35–66 (Apocrypha*)

Benedictus (Latin = Blessed) The canticle* which begins 'Blessed be the Lord God of Israel'. (Morning Prayer*) C.W.* 'Blessed be the Lord the God of Israel'. Luke* 1.68–79, the Song of Zechariah at the birth of his son, John the Baptist.

Gloria Patri (Latin = Glory to the Father) The ending which is used at the end of all canticles* (except Te Deum*) and at the end of psalms*. BCP* – 'Glory be to the Father, and to the Son, and to the Holy Ghost. As it was in the beginning, is now and ever shall be, world without end. Amen'. C.W.* – 'Glory to the Father and to the Son, and to the Holy Spirit; as it was in the beginning, is now, and shall be for ever. Amen'.

Jubilate Deo (Latin = O be joyful in the Lord) The canticle* which begins 'O be joyful in the Lord, all ye lands'. (Morning Prayer*) C.W.* 'O be joyful in the Lord all the earth'. Psalm* 100.

Magnificat (Latin = Magnifies) The canticle* which begins 'My soul doth magnify the Lord'. (Evening Prayer*) C.W.* 'My soul proclaims the greatness of the Lord'. Luke 1.46–55, the Song of the Blessed Virgin Mary.

Nunc Dimittis (Latin = Now let depart) The canticle* which begins 'Now lettest thou thy servant depart in peace'. (Evening Prayer*) C.W.* 'Now, Lord, you let your servant go in peace.' Luke 2.29–32. The Song of Simeon on seeing the infant Christ.

Te Deum (Latin = Thee O God) The canticle* which begins 'We praise thee, O God, we acknowledge thee to be the Lord'. (Morning Prayer*) C.W.* 'We praise you, O God, we acclaim you as the Lord.' Generally thought to be the work of Niceta, Bishop of Remesiana, died c. A.D. 414.

Veni Creator (Latin – Come, Creator) The first words of a hymn* to the Holy Spirit* – 'Come, Holy Ghost, our souls inspire' – probably composed in the 9th. century. Used in the Church of England* at Pentecost*, in the B.C.P* and C.W.* Ordinals*, and sometimes at Confirmations* and the consecration* of churches*.

Venite (Latin = O Come) The canticle* which begins 'O come, let us sing out to the Lord'. (Morning prayer*) C.W.* 'O come, let us sing to the Lord'. Psalm* 95.

3 Music for the Eucharist*

Agnus Dei (Latin = Lamb of God) The anthem* said or sung either as part of the Gloria in excelsis* or before or during the Communion (C.W.*). BCP* – 'Lamb of God . . . that takest away the sins of the world'. C.W.* – 'Lamb of God, you take away the sin of the world' or 'Jesus, Lamb of God'.

Benedictus qui venit (Latin – Blessed he who comes) The anthem* which may be said or sung during the course of the C.W.* Eucharistic* Prayer. 'Blessed is he who comes in the Name of the Lord'.

Credo (Latin = I believe) The Nicene Creed*.

Gloria in excelsis Deo (Latin = Glory to God in the highest) The anthem* which is said or sung at the end (BCP) or near the beginning (C.W.*) of the Eucharist*. BCP* – 'Glory be to God on high', C.W.* – 'Glory to God in the highest'. It is generally omitted in Advent* and Lent* and on days which are not principal festivals, though the BCP does not allow its omission at any time.

Kyrie Eleison (Greek = Lord, have mercy) The litany* which may be used near the beginning of the C.W.* Eucharist*. It frequently replaces the Gloria* in Advent* and Lent*.

Sanctus (Latin = holy) The anthem* said or sung during the course of the Eucharistic* Prayer. BCP – 'Holy, holy, holy, Lord God of hosts'. C.W.* – 'Holy, holy, holy Lord, God of power and might'.

Sursum Corda (Latin = lift up hearts) The words which are said or sung at the beginning of the Eucharistic* Prayer – 'Lift up your hearts'.

8 The Church's Year

A WORD OF EXPLANATION

The Church's Year has a well-defined pattern. It is split into two parts. The first part runs from Advent Sunday* to Trinity Sunday*. In the first part of the Church's Year, we hear of God's preparations for the revelation* of himself in Jesus Christ*, the Birth, Life, Ministry, Death, Resurrection* and Ascension* of Christ, the coming of the Holy Spirit* to the disciples*, and the way all this is expressed in a Trinitarian* faith. The second part of the Church's Year, which covers the Sundays after Trinity*, up to twenty-two in all, and the Sundays before Advent*, is a time when we try to absorb the implications of Christ's teaching, with its many-faceted themes.

Some of the Church's seasons* vary in length. For example, the number of Sundays after Christmas* depends on the day of the week on which the Feast* of the Epiphany* (6 January) falls, the number of Sundays before Lent* depends on the Sunday on which Easter* falls, the number of Sundays in the Trinity season again depends on the Sunday on which Easter falls. The principal cause of the variations is the date of Easter. The events of the Cross* and the Resurrection* took place at the time of the Jewish Passover* Festival, when the Jews commemorated (and still commemorate) the Exodus*. The Passover meal was kept at the time of the full moon, on the night of 14–15 Nisan, whatever the day of the week on which it happened to fall. After much controversy in earlier centuries, the date of Easter was fixed on the Sunday following the Passover full moon. Because of the moon's involvement, the festival is obviously movable and, in our own calendar, can take place on the relevant Sunday between 22 March and 25 April. There have been moves to fix the date of Easter on the third Sunday in April, but, although the Churches of the West are in agreement, the Eastern Churches are unwilling to accept the change.

Apart from the general structure of the Church's Year, there are many special holy days and saints' days (see subsections 1, 2 & 3 of this Section).

In *The Christian Year: Calendar, Lectionary and Collects* (Church House Publishing), the psalms* and readings are based on a three-year cycle. In the year (Advent to Advent) 1999–2000, the psalms and readings for Year B are used, in 2000–2001 Year C, in 2001–2002 Year A and so on.

Seasons* and special days are marked by the use of different colours* for altar hangings*, vestments*, etc. Although there are variations in the colours which may be used on certain occasions, the standard four are white, purple, green and red. These colours are indicated in the text, and are known as the liturgical colours.

1 The General Calendar

Sundays of Advent – 1st, 2nd, 3rd, 4th – Purple
(Advent – Latin – *adventus* – coming) A time of preparation, not only for the coming of Christ at Christmas*, but also for the Second Coming of Christ as Judge at the Last Day (see **Parousia**). As a consequence, the Advent themes are often called the Last Things – death, hell, heaven, judgement (see relevant entries).

Christmas Eve – 24 December – Purple
A day of preparation for Christmas Day*.

CHRISTMAS DAY – 25 December – White
First major festival – Principal Holy Day (Christmas = Christ Mass, i.e. the mass* held to celebrate the Birth of Christ). The corruption 'Xmas' derives from the fact that the Greek letter for 'Ch' (the first two letters of 'Christ') is 'X' (*chi*). The date of Christ's Birth is not known. The custom of keeping the feast on 25 December is first mentioned in the Roman Philocalian Calendar of A.D. 336. This date was probably chosen to oppose the pagan feast of *Dies Natalis Solis Invicti* (the birth of the unconquered sun – a winter festival) by the celebration of the birth of the 'Sun of Righteousness'. In the Armenian Church, 6 January (Epiphany*) is still observed as Christmas Day.

Sundays of Christmas – 1st, (2nd) – White
If Christmas Day falls on Wednesday, Thursday, Friday or Saturday, there will be two Sundays after Christmas.

Epiphany – 6 January – White – Principal Holy Day
(Greek – *epiphaneia* – manifestation, showing forth) Originally the feast was held in honour of our Lord's Baptism, and still is in the Eastern Church. In the West, it became associated with the showing of Christ to the Gentile* world, in the persons of the Wise Men. (see **Magi** and see also **Sundays of the Epiphany**). No number of Wise Men is given in the New Testament*, but the three gifts presented – gold, frankincense and myrrh – have led to the assumption that there were three. Nowhere is it suggested that they were Kings.
    When a Christmas crib* is used, the figures of the Wise Men are added on the Eve of the Epiphany.

Sundays of the Epiphany – 1st, 2nd, 3rd, 4th – White. The principal title of the First Sunday of the Epiphany is the Baptism* of Christ, which serves to unite Eastern and Western traditions (see **Epiphany**). This season ends on the 40th day after Christmas with the Feast of the Presentation of Christ in the Temple (Candlemas) on 2 February (see **Special Days**, subsection 3 of this Section).

Sundays before Lent – up to five, the last being the Sunday next before Lent – Green. A change in emphasis as the Church's most solemn season* of preparation approaches. A transitional period between the joy of Christmas* and the Epiphany* and the more serious themes of Lent*. The three Sundays immediately before Lent are known in the BCP* as Septuagesima, Sexagesima, and Quinquagesima (Latin –

seventieth, sixtieth and fiftieth) i.e. 70, approx. 60, and approx. 50 days before Easter*.

Shrove Tuesday – the day before Lent – Green (corruption of 'shrive' – the act of being 'shriven' entailed making confession* of sin* and receiving absolution* from a priest*). Also known as Pancake Day. On this day, in former times, the faithful were accustomed to make their confession, in preparation for Lent*, and since the season was one of fasting*, they would get rid of fat, flour, eggs etc. by making pancakes.

Ash Wednesday – the first day of Lent – Purple or Lent array

Principal Holy Day. ('Lent' is derived from the Old German *Lenz* – Spring). The first day of Lent, 40 days (not counting the Sundays) or six and a half weeks before Easter*. The word 'Ash' derives from the custom of using ash as a sign of mourning or penitence* (cf. Old Testament* – 'sackcloth and ashes'). In many churches, the palms from the previous year's Palm Sunday* are burned, and, with the ash, the sign of the Cross* is made on the foreheads of the faithful at the Eucharist* on Ash Wednesday.

Sundays of Lent – 1st, 2nd, 3rd, 4th, 5th, 6th – Purple (Red on Palm Sunday*) or Lent array

During this season the faithful follow our Lord from the wilderness to the Cross*, sharing the lessons of his temptations, his conflicts, and his sufferings.

> **Lent 4** is also known as Mothering Sunday, Refreshment Sunday, Mid-Lent Sunday and *Laetare* Sunday. The name 'Mothering' derives from *either* the custom in former times of apprentices or others visiting their mothers on this day *or* the practice of visiting the cathedral* or mother church on this day *or* the words in the Epistle* for the day (BCP*) 'Jerusalem, which is the mother of us all'. The name 'Refreshment' derives from *either* the story of the feeding of the five thousand which is the Gospel* for the day (BCP) *or* the relaxation of Lenten discipline allowed on this day (e.g. simnel-cakes were eaten). The name 'Mid-Lent' is self-explanatory though approximate. The name *Laetare* is the Latin for 'Rejoice ye' – the first two words of the Introit* (Isaiah* 66.10) used at the Eucharist* on that day, and indicates again a relaxation of Lenten discipline.

> **Lent 5** is known as Passion Sunday in BCP* (Latin – *passio* – suffering). It marks the beginning of the two weeks of Passiontide, during which the Church commemorates the sufferings of our Lord during the last days of his earthly life. During Passiontide, in many churches, crucifixes*, pictures and statues are veiled in purple. Since 1969 the Roman Catholic Church has discontinued the title and combined its observance with that of Palm Sunday*. The new Calendar denotes it as the Fifth Sunday of Lent, but adds, 'Passiontide begins'.

> **Lent 6** is also known as Palm Sunday and marks the beginning of **Holy Week**, which is a time of special devotion to the Passion* of

Christ. Palm Sunday commemorates the triumphal entry of Christ into Jerusalem when, according to the Gospel* narrative, people strewed branches of palm in his path. It is marked in many churches by the blessing and distribution of palm crosses, and, in some churches, by a solemn procession*. In medieval times Palm Sunday was called 'Yew Sunday', because branches of yew were carried in procession.

Monday, Tuesday and Wednesday of Holy Week Red, Purple or Lent array

Maundy Thursday Red, Purple or Lent array, but White at Holy Communion* – Principal Holy Day.

(Latin – *mandatum* – command) The name derives from the *mandatum novum* – the new commandment to love one another – given to his disciples* at the Last Supper by our Lord in the night in which he was betrayed and on the day before he was crucified*. In addition to this new commandment, our Lord demonstrated to the disciples their utter dependence on him and their calling as servants by washing their feet. During the Supper, he commanded them to break the bread and eat, to bless the cup and drink in remembrance of him, sharing thereby in his Body and Blood, soon to be broken and poured out on the Cross*. In this way the Eucharist* was instituted and has been celebrated ever since in the Christian Church. In many churches a Eucharist is celebrated in the evening of Maundy Thursday. In some churches the ceremony of the Washing of Feet takes place during evening Eucharist after the sermon*. Another custom on Maundy Thursday is the blessing of the Holy Oils* in the cathedral* church, together, in many dioceses*, with a re-affirmation of vows by the clergy*. To symbolise the sovereign's* role as servant, the sovereign distributes Maundy money to members of the laity* on this day.

Maundy Thursday is also known as Sheer ('clean') Thursday, and, in Germany, is known as Green Thursday from the custom of providing those who made their confession* on Ash Wednesday* with green branches on Maundy Thursday to symbolise the completion of their penance*.

Good Friday Red, but, more commonly, all hangings (frontals* etc) are removed – Principal Holy Day.

The day of our Lord's Crucifixion*. It is known as 'Good' because, on that day, Jesus Christ achieved the salvation* of the human race.

Easter Eve (Holy Saturday) Hangings removed. Day of Preparation.

The day commemorates the resting of Christ's body in the tomb. In many churches a service of Ante-Communion* is held early in the day and the Easter Vigil* is observed during the evening or night. The Vigil consists of readings from both Old and New Testaments*, the blessing of the new fire, the marking of the Paschal* candle, the lighting of the candle, its solemn procession* through the church during which the candles of the people are lit from it, and the Light of Christ proclaimed, the recitation of the *Exultet* (or Easter Song of Praise), the blessing of the baptismal* water, and the re-making of the baptismal vows by the faithful.

EASTER DAY – White or Gold – Second, but greatest, of the major festivals – Principal Holy Day.

(The name probably derives from the feast day of *Eostre*, an Anglo-Saxon pagan spring goddess.) For the date of Easter see the introduction to this Section.

The Feast of the Resurrection* of Christ, the day on which Christ's followers found his tomb empty, is the greatest and oldest feast of the Christian Church*. Christ rose from the dead 'on the third day' after his Crucifixion*. The 'third' day is Sunday – and not Monday as our present method of calculation would suggest – because, in our Lord's time, the day on which an event happened, i.e. in this case, Friday, was counted as the first day. Because Sunday is the Day of Resurrection*, the Church thinks of every Sunday as being a little Easter Day, and, consequently, a day of worship*, rest and recreation.

Monday to Saturday in Easter Week White

Sundays of Easter 2nd, 3rd, 4th, 5th. 6th, 7th (Sunday after Ascension Day) – White

> **Easter 2** is also known as Low Sunday, as a contrast to the 'high' day the previous Sunday.
>
> **Easter 6** is sometimes known as Rogation Sunday (Latin *rogare* – to ask). The 'Major Rogation' was kept in former times on 25 April when the faithful processed through the cornfields to pray for the preservation of the crops from mildew. The 'Minor Rogations' – the Monday, Tuesday and Wednesday before Ascension Day – are days which derived from the processional litanies ordered by Bishop Mamertus (c. A.D. 470) of Vienne in Gaul when his diocese* was troubled by volcanic eruptions. The practice of Rogation processions* and the blessing of the crops still persists in many rural parishes.

Rogation Monday, Tuesday and Wednesday – White – Special Days of Prayer (see **Easter 6**)

ASCENSION DAY – White – Third major festival – Principal Holy Day.

(Latin – *ascendere* – to go up) The withdrawal of Christ into heaven*, witnessed by the Apostles*. The Ascension marked the end of the post-Resurrection* appearances of Christ and his return in triumph to take his place at God's right hand from where he reigns in glory*. Just as there are 40 days (not counting the Sundays) between Ash Wednesday* and Easter Day*, so the Ascension falls 40 days after Easter. These latter days are sometimes known as the Great Forty Days.

The concept of Christ going 'up' derives from the understanding of the structure of the universe common in our Lord's day, with the earth a table supported on pillars, topped by the arc of the firmament (the sun, moon, stars, etc.), and heaven above them. So our Lord's contemporaries would inevitably think of his return to heaven as taking an upward direction.

PENTECOST – Red – Fourth major festival – Principal Holy Day
(Greek – *pentecoste* – fiftieth. The Greek name for the Feast of Weeks
– the Jewish feast of the first fruits of the corn harvest – which fell
fifty days after the Passover*.) The day on which the Holy Spirit*
descended on the disciples* (Acts* 2.1ff), sometimes called the birthday
of the Church. It is also known as Whit Sunday or White Sunday,
because it was common practice to baptise* on that day, which enjoined
the use of white robes.

Trinity Sunday White on this day only.
A feast in honour of the Holy Trinity, embracing God in all three
Persons, Father, Son and Holy Spirit. It serves to summarise the whole
story of God's revelation* and concludes the first half of the Church's
Year (see also **Trinity**).

Sundays after Trinity – Green
The second half of the Church's Year with the Sundays before Advent.
See the introduction to this section.

Sundays before Advent – Four are possible. Green
The title of the last of these (viz. the Sunday next before Advent) is
Christ the King and is a fitting climax to the liturgical* cycle and
celebrates the reality of God's rule and of the final ingathering into his
kingdom.

2 Festivals and Lesser Festivals

A list of Festivals and Lesser Festivals can be found on pages 23–34 of *The
Christian Year: Calendar, Lectionary & Collects*. The liturgical* colour*
for these days is usually either red or white.

3 Special Days

Feast of the Presentation of Christ in the Temple (Candlemas)
White – Principal Holy Day – 2 February (BCP* – the Purification of
the Blessed Virgin Mary). Candlemas = Candle mass (see **Sundays of
the Epiphany**). On this day, it is customary in some churches to light
candles whilst the *Nunc Dimittis** is being sung at Evening Prayer*.
They are then carried in procession* to commemorate the carrying of
Christ, the True Light, into the Temple at Jerusalem.

Feast of the Annunciation of our Lord to the Blessed Virgin Mary Gold
or white – Principal Holy Day – 25 March (Lady Day)

All Saints' Day – Gold or white – Principal Holy Day – 1 November

Ember Days (Old English – *ymbryne* – period)
Liturgical* colour* of the season*.
Either the Wednesdays, Fridays and Saturdays in the weeks before the
third Sunday of Advent*, the 2nd Sunday of Lent*, and the Sundays
nearest to the festivals of St Peter and St Paul (29 June) and St Michael

and All Angels (29 September) *or* in the week before a bishop* holds an Ordination*. On these days prayers are offered for all who serve the Church* in its ministries*, both clerical* and lay*, and for all who are to be ordained* or commissioned for those ministries.

4 Days of discipline and self-denial

Ash Wednesday*, the weekdays of Lent*, Good Friday*. All Fridays except those falling on Christmas Day*, the Epiphany*, Festivals* and the Fridays from Easter Day* to Pentecost*.

5 Other Days

Patronal Festival The feast* day kept on the day of the saint* after whom the church* is named i.e. the patron saint.

Corpus Christi (Latin – Body of Christ) The Thursday after Trinity Sunday*. A day of thanksgiving for the institution* of Holy Communion*.

Lammas Day (= Loaf mass*) 1 August. In earlier times, it was customary at the Eucharist* on this day to use bread made from the first-ripe corn of the harvest.

Michaelmas (mas = mass*) 29 September. Another name for the feast and octave* of St Michael and All Angels.

Harvest Thanksgiving Usually in September or October. A day of thanksgiving for the fruits of the harvest.

Feast of Dedication The Dedication Festival* of a church*, which is the anniversary of the date of its dedication (setting aside for public worship*) or consecration*. If the actual date is not known, the festival may be kept on the first Sunday* in October.

Remembrance Sunday The Sunday nearest 11 November, on which those who have died in wars in the service of their country are remembered.

Eve of St Andrew 29 November. A day of prayer and thanksgiving for the missionary* work of the Church.

6 Other words

Calendar (Latin – *kalendae* – the first day of the month) The table of Sundays, festivals, lesser festivals, special days and other days which forms the pattern of the Church's Year (see introduction to this Section).

Holiday An abbreviation of 'holy day'. In former times, rest from work took place on the Church's holy days. Although some holidays still coincide with the Church's festivals (e.g. Christmas*, Easter*), the word now has a more general application.

Lectionary (Latin – *legere* – to read) *Either* a book containing the extracts from the Scriptures* to be read at public worship* in accordance with the Church's Calendar *or* a tabulated list of those extracts.

Movable feasts Ecclesiastical* feasts* which do not fall on a fixed date in the secular* calendar, but vary according to determined rules e.g. Easter Day*, Ascension Day*, Pentecost*, Advent Sunday*.

Octave (Latin – *octava* – eighth) The eighth day after a festival, reckoned inclusively, so that the octave always falls on the same day of the week as the festival itself. It probably derives from the Old Testament* custom of maintaining a festival through eight days (e.g. the Feast of Tabernacles – Leviticus* 23.36; the Dedication of the Temple – 2 Chronicles* 7.9).

Season (Old French – *seson*) A period in the Church's Year* e.g. the season of Lent*, the Easter* season.

9 At the Eucharist

A WORD OF EXPLANATION

The order of service used in this explanation is that of Order One in C.W.*

The principal service of the Church*, the Eucharist*, falls naturally into two parts. The first part of the service, after a time of preparation which includes Prayers* of Penitence*, might be called the Bible Class, because, it is based on the reading and the proclamation of the Good News, revealed both in the Old and New Testaments*. So we find in this part an Old Testament reading, a psalm* from the Old Testament's Psalter*, a reading from the New Testament Letters (the Epistle*), and a reading from one of the four Gospels* in the New Testament. A sermon* is preached, usually based on a text from one of the readings, and is followed by the saying or singing of the Nicene Creed*, which summarises the faith* expressed in what has gone before. The Prayers of Intercession* complete the first part of the service.

The second part of the service, from the Giving of the Peace* to the Dismissal*, is the Lord's Supper*. Its focal point is the taking, the blessing and the sharing of the bread* and wine*, whereby Christ comes to his Family through his Real Presence* in the Body and Blood of the Eucharist. The Church has followed our Lord's command to 'Do this, in remembrance of me' from the moment he instituted* the sacrament* at the Last Supper on Maundy Thursday* night.

Ablutions (Latin – *ablutio* – washing) The washing of the celebrant's* fingers and the chalice* immediately after the Communion* in the Eucharist*. The custom became established in the tenth or eleventh century. After the Communion, wine* is poured over the celebrant's fingers into the chalice and drunk and then wine and water follow, together with the pouring of water onto the paten*. Often today the ablutions are done in water only. The practice serves as a reminder of the sacred nature of the elements*.

Absolution (Latin – *absolutio* – acquittal) The formal act of a priest* or bishop* pronouncing the forgiveness* of sins* by God to those who are qualified by repentance* to receive it (see also **Mediator** and **Redeemer**). Absolution may be pronounced during an act of public worship*, or privately as part of Sacramental Confession*.

Acolyte (Greek – *akalouthos* – follower) In the Church of England*, acolytes are those who light the altar* candle, and carry candles in procession* (see also **Server**).

Agape (Greek – *agape* – love) The common religious meal which was held in the early Church either before or later than the Eucharist*, with which it ought not to be confused.

Alms (Greek – *eleemosune* – compassionateness) Gifts of money collected during public worship from the congregation* strictly speaking for the relief of the poor. They should be distinguished from 'dues', which is money collected to maintain the services, staff and fabric of a church. Both are now covered by the general word 'collection'*.

Altar The place on which the Eucharist* is celebrated.

Altar book The book which contains the order(s) of service, collects*, readings and music* for the Eucharist* throughout the year (see **Missal**).

Altar cloth The cloth, usually of linen, which covers the top of an altar* and hangs down at both sides. It is also known as the fair linen cloth.

Anamnesis (Greek – memorial) The word used in the narrative of the Lord's Supper* in the New Testament* cf. **Luke*** 22.19, **1 Corinthians*** 11.24 – 'do this in **remembrance** of me'. Liturgical* scholars see it as denoting the commemoration of the Passion*, Resurrection* and Ascension* of Christ* which, in C.W.* Order One, Eucharistic Prayer A comes in the Words of Institution* In English 'remembrance' suggests that the person or deed commemorated is past and absent, whereas, in this context, it signifies an objective act in and by which the person or event commemorated is actually made present and brought into the here and now.

Anaphora (Greek – offering) The central prayer* in the Eucharistic* Liturgy* which contains the Consecration*, the Anamnesis* and the Communion*.

Ante-Communion (Latin – *ante* – before. See **Holy Communion**). That part of the Eucharist* up to and including the Intercession* (C.W.*) (or Prayer for the Church Militant BCP*) It is not a Eucharist. It is often used on Good Friday* and Easter Eve*. It can be used when a priest* is not available to celebrate*. Its only real parallel in ancient times is the Mass of the Catechumens*.

Asperges (Latin – *aspergere* – sprinkle) The ceremony of sprinkling holy water over the altar* and people before the principal Eucharist* on Sundays*. During the ceremony, a chant from psalm* 51 may be used – '*Asperges me, Domine*' – Sprinkle me, Lord'.

Benediction (Latin – *bene* – well, *dicere* – to speak) A service usually held in the afternoon or evening which culminates in the blessing of the people with the Reserved Sacrament* in a monstrance* or veiled ciborium*.

Blessed Sacrament (see **Sacrament**) A term used of the Sacrament of the Eucharist*, applied both to the service itself, and more especially to the consecrated elements*.

Blessing, The The words spoken by the celebrant* at the end of the Eucharist* assuring the congregation* of God's favour.

Both kinds The custom of receiving both the bread* and the wine* in Holy Communion*.

Bowing A bending of the head or body in reverence. From very early times, Christians have bowed when the name of Jesus is mentioned. There is also the widespread custom of bowing to the altar* when entering or leaving a church*.

Bread (see **Unleavened Bread**)

Burse (Latin – *bursa* – bag) A case consisting of two squares of stiffened material, joined along one or three sides, in which the corporal* is kept. It is often embroidered, and can agree with the liturgical colour* of the season* or day (see **Veil**).

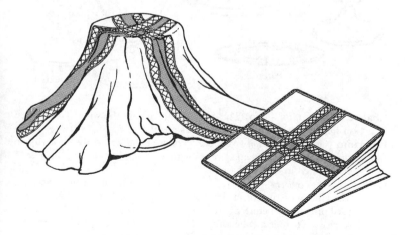

A Burse and Veil

Canon of the Mass (Greek – *kanon* – rule) That part of the Eucharist* which is called the Eucharistic Prayer or Prayer of Consecration. Its contents vary in different liturgies*, but always contain the Words of Institution*.

Celebrant (Latin – *celebrare* – to celebrate) The bishop or priest* who officiates at the Eucharist*. Verb: celebrate.

Censer (Latin – *incensum* – thing burnt) The vessel in which incense* is burnt (see **Thurible**).

Ceremonial (Latin – *caerimonialis* – of a ceremony) The prescribed and formal actions used during Divine worship*.

Ciborium

Chalice

Paten

Cruets

Chalice (Latin – *calix* – cup) The cup used to contain the wine* consecrated in the Eucharist*, often of precious metal.

Ciborium (Greek – *kiborion* – the seed-vessel of the water lily, or a cup so shaped) A chalice*-shaped vessel with a lid, used to contain the bread* consecrated in the Eucharist*.

Collect (Latin – *collecta* – collected, summed up) The short form of prayer*, basically consisting of an invocation*, a petition* and an ascription*, used principally before the readings in the Eucharist*, but also in other services. There is a collect for each Sunday of the Church's year*, and for all special days and occasions. The name derives from *either* a prayer said when the people of God are collected together *or* a prayer which collects or sums up the theme of the day.

Collection (Latin – *collectio* – collection) The collecting of money during a church service (see **Alms**).

Comfortable Words Four passages from the New Testament* (**Matthew***
11.28, **John*** 3.16, **1 Timothy*** 1.15, **1 John*** 2.1) which the celebrant*
at Holy Communion* recites (B.C.P.*), may recite (C.W.* Order Two)
after the Absolution* to confirm God's forgiveness* for the believer.

Communicant One who receives Holy Communion*.

Concelebration The joint celebration of the Eucharist* by a number of priests
reciting the central parts of the Eucharistic Prayer (Prayer of Consecration) together.

Confession (Latin – *confessio* – confession) The acknowledgement of sin*
made publicly by a congregation* during the course of the Eucharist*,
and also in other services. (see also **Sacramental Confession**)

Consecration (Latin – *consecratio* – the act of setting apart as sacred) The
means whereby, by word and action, the bread* and wine* of the
Eucharist* are set apart as sacred and sacramentally become the Body
and Blood of Christ. (see also Sections 3 & 6)

Corporal (Medieval Latin – *corporalis* – body cloth) The square linen cloth,
placed on the altar cloth*, in the centre of the altar*, on which the
bread* and wine* for the Eucharist* are placed. A second corporal can
be used to cover the chalice* during the Eucharist (see also **Pall**)

Creed (Latin – *credo* – I believe) The confession of faith* known as the Nicene
Creed* which is said or sung during the Eucharist*. (see Section 11)

Cross, sign of the (Latin – *crux* – cross) From earliest times, an act of
Christian devotion made at particular points during the Eucharist* (and
at other times both inside and outside the church) to remind the faithful
of their dependence on Christ and his Cross*. It is made by drawing
the right hand from forehead to breast and then from left shoulder to
right shoulder, completing the act by returning the hand to the centre.

Cruets The vessels of glass, precious metal or earthenware in which the wine*
and water* for the Eucharist* are brought to the altar*.

Deacon (Greek – *diakonos* – servant) In some churches, the Eucharist* is
celebrated by Priest*, Deacon* and Sub-Deacon*. Although originally
the ministers celebrating were in the Orders so named, today the function of Deacon or Sub-Deacon is often carried out by a Priest or Deacon.
The 'Deacon', in this sense, reads or sings the Gospel*, presents the
elements* to the celebrant*, invites the congregation* to pray, and says
or sings the words of Dismissal* at the end of the Eucharist. (see
Section 3)

Dismissal (Latin – *dismissus* – sent away) The words used at the end of the
Eucharist* to dismiss the people, i.e. to send them out having been
fortified with the Body and Blood of Christ.

Elements (Latin – *elementum* – part) The bread* and wine* of the Eucharist*.

Elevation (Latin – *elevare* – to lift) The holding up of the Host* in the
Eucharist* for the faithful to see and reverence. (see also Section 6)

Epiklesis (Greek – *epi* – upon, *kaleo* – call) The petition* in the Eucharist*
invoking the Father to send the Holy Spirit* upon the bread* and
wine* so that they may become sacramentally* the Body and Blood of
Christ, e.g. C.W.* Order One, Eucharistic Prayer A: 'grant that by the

power of your Holy Spirit these gifts of bread and wine may be to us his body and his blood'. (see also **Invocation**)

Epistle (Greek – *epistole* – sent: Latin – *epistola* – letter) The passage of Scripture*, usually an extract from one of the letters appearing in the New Testament*, but also sometimes from the Book of the Acts of the Apostles* or from the Revelation of St John the Divine*, which is the reading which comes before the Gospel* reading in the Eucharist*.

Epistoler The person who reads the Epistle* at the Eucharist*.

Eucharist (Greek – *eukharistia* – grateful offering) An alternative name for the Holy Communion*, the Lord's Supper*, or the Mass*. The title is to be explained *either* by the fact that, at the Last Supper, Christ 'gave thanks', *or* by the fact that it is the supreme act of Christian thanksgiving.

Exposition (Latin – *exponere* – expose) The exhibition of the consecrated* Eucharistic* host* for the purpose of devotion by the faithful (cf. **Benediction**).

Fair linen cloth (see **Altar cloth**)

Fast   A day or days of abstinence (now used in the Church of England* more in the sense of 'preparation'). These include the seasons of Advent* and Lent*, the days before the great festivals, and Ember Days*. The practices of keeping Friday, the Day of the Cross*, as a fast day by eating fish, and of fasting before receiving Communion* are still maintained by some.

Ferial (Latin – *feria* – holiday) The meaning of the word has been totally reversed. 'Ferial' is now applied to those days (apart from Saturdays and Sundays) on which no feast falls, i.e. an 'ordinary' day.

Flagon A large vessel, usually with handles, spout and lid, often of precious metal, used to hold the wine* for the Eucharist*.

Fraction (Latin – *fractum* – broken) The breaking of the bread* at the Eucharist* before the Communion*. It mirrors the third of the four actions performed by our Lord at the Last Supper – 'he took, he blessed, he broke, he gave'.

Genuflection (Latin – *genu* – knee, *flectere* – bend) The act of bending the right knee during the Eucharist* and before the Blessed Sacrament* as a sign of devotion.

Gospel (Old English – *god spel* – good tidings) The extract from one of the four Gospels* in the New Testament* (Matthew*, Mark*, Luke*, John*) read during the Eucharist* after the Epistle*.

Gospeller The person who reads the Gospel* at the Eucharist*.

Gradual (Latin – *gradus* – step) The psalm*, part of a psalm or hymn* sung between the Epistle* and Gospel* at the Eucharist*. The name derives from the practice of singing the Gradual on the altar* steps, or whilst the deacon* was ascending the steps of the ambo*.

High Mass In some churches, used to denote the principal Eucharist* on Sundays and the greater feasts. Its essential feature is the presence of deacon* and sub-deacon* assisting the celebrant*; they are accompanied by the choir*, the thurifer*, and a number of servers* or acolytes*.

Other distinctive features are the use of incense* and the giving of the Pax*. (see **Mass**).

Holy Communion (German – *heilig* – sacred. Communion = Common Union.) An alternative name for the Eucharist*, the Lord's Supper* or the Mass*, and also the act of receiving the bread* and wine* at the Eucharist.

Holy table An alternative word for altar*.

Host (Latin – *hostia* – victim) The word originally meant a sacrificial victim and so, by derivation, the consecrated bread* in the Eucharist* is regarded as the Sacrifice* of the Body of Christ.

Humble Access, Prayer of In the BCP*, the prayer which immediately precedes the Prayer of Consecration* in the service of Holy Communion*. In C.W.* Eucharist* Order One, it may be said immediately before the distribution of Communion.' Its opening words are: 'We do not presume to come to this thy (your) table, merciful Lord'.

Incense (Latin – *incensum* – a thing burnt) A kind of gum which, when specially treated, gives off a sweet smell when burnt. It is used in some churches, being burnt in a censer*. The burning of incense to God or a god is an ancient tradition often mentioned in the Old Testament*. The 'sweet smell' was considered an acceptable offering – the rising smoke is symbolic of prayers* rising to God. An alternative name for incense is frankincense – one of the three gifts brought to the Infant Jesus by the Wise Men. (see **Epiphany**)

Institution, Words of (Latin – *instituere* – to set up) The words used by Jesus Christ at the Last Supper as he broke the bread and blessed the cup, enjoining his disciples to 'do this in remembrance of me'. (see **Maundy Thursday**) Thereby he established the Eucharist* as the supreme act identifying the Christian community.

Intercession (Latin – *intercedere* – to intervene – by derivation *intercessio*) The prayers of petition* on behalf of others which follow the Creed* in the Eucharist*, although intercessory prayers form part of almost all Christian worship*.

Intinction (Latin – *tingere* – to stain) The dipping of the Eucharistic bread* in the wine*, or the placing of a spot of wine on the Eucharistic wafer*, to enable communicants*, especially sick communicants, to receive both species* at once.

Introit (Latin – *introire* – to go in) A psalm*, hymn* or other words sung as the priest* approaches the altar* to celebrate the Eucharist*.

Kiss of Peace (Latin – *pax* – peace) The greeting exchanged by the faithful before the elements* of the Eucharist* are laid on the altar*. The greeting was originally a kiss but has been modified either to the enclosing of one person's hands within those of another person, or to a handshake. The greeting is accompanied by the words: 'The peace of the Lord be always with you' or 'The peace of the Lord' or 'Peace be with you'.

Lavabo (Latin – *lavabo* – I will wash [Psalm* 26.6]) The washing of the celebrant's* hands at the completing of the Offertory* in the Eucharist*. The act is usually performed by a server*.

Lavabo dish The dish into which the water used for the lavabo* is poured.

Lavabo towel The towel used to wipe the celebrant's* hands at the lavabo*.

Liturgy (Greek – *leitourgia: laos* – people, *ergos* – working) The word was originally used of a public duty of any kind. It eventually came to be used *either* specifically as a name for the Eucharist*, the chief act of public worship*, *or* as an inclusive word to cover all the prescribed services of the Church*.

Lord's Supper An alternative name for the Eucharist*, Holy Communion* or Mass*.

Low Mass (see **High Mass**) A simple celebration of the Eucharist* without elaborate ceremonial*. The name is applied to any Eucharist on Sundays or greater festivals apart from the principal one, and to a week-day Eucharist.

Manual acts (Latin – *manus* – hand) The rubrics* in the B.C,P,* Holy Communion* service require that, at the consecration*, the paten* should be taken into the celebrant's hands, who should break the bread*, lay hands upon it, performing corresponding acts at the consecration of the wine*. Similarly in C.W.* Order Two. In C.W.* Order One the president takes the bread and wine before the Eucharistic Prayer* and may also use the traditional acts in the course of the Prayer.'

Mass (Latin – *missa* from *mittere* – to send) An alternative name for the Eucharist*, Holy Communion* or Lord's Supper*.

Mass of the Presanctified (Latin – *prae* – before, *sacer* – holy) The Eucharistic* service without the Consecration*. Bread and wine which have been consecrated at an earlier service are used for Communion*. In the Church of England* this service is held in some churches, usually only on Good Friday*.

Missal (Latin – *liber* – book, *missalis* – of the Mass) The book which contains the order(s) of service, collects*, readings and music* for the Eucharist* throughout the year (see **Altar book**).

Monstrance (Latin – *monstrare* – to show) A frame with gold or silver rays in the centre of which is a receptacle with a glass window. The Host* is placed in the receptacle and displayed to the congregation*, usually at the service of Benediction*.

North side The practice of celebrating the Eucharist* at the north side of the altar*, as opposed to the more customary eastward or westward positions.

Nuptial Mass (Latin – *nuptiae* – wedding) A celebration of the Eucharist*, immediately following a marriage*.

Oblations (Late Latin – *oblationes* – offerings) The offerings made during the course of the Eucharist*.

Offertory (Ecclesiastical Latin – *offertorium* – offering) The bringing to, or presentation at the altar* of the bread* and wine* to be consecrated in the Eucharist*. The Offertory or Preparation of the Table follows the giving of the Peace* in C.W.* and is often combined with the offering of the collection*.

Old Testament lesson The first of the three readings now common at the Eucharist*.

Ordinary of the Mass (Latin *Ordo Missae*) The parts of the Eucharist* which do not vary, i.e. the basic structure of the service (see **Proper**).

Pall (Latin – *pallium* – cloak) At the Eucharist* a stiffened linen square used to cover the chalice*.

Paten (Latin – *patena* – a shallow basin) The dish, often of precious metal, on which the bread* is placed at the Eucharist*.

Pax (See **Kiss of Peace**)

Preface (Latin – *prae* – before, *fari* – speak) In the Eucharist*, the words which introduce the central part of the service. It begins with the Sursum Corda* and ends with the Sanctus*. It is the giving of praise to God in union with the whole Church* on earth and in heaven*.

President (Latin – *prae* – before, *sedere* – to sit) A priest*, or a bishop* if present, presides over the Eucharist*. The President says the opening greeting, the collect*, the absolution*, the Peace*, takes the bread and cup, says the Eucharistic prayer (or Prayer of Consecration*), breaks the consecrated bread, receives the sacrament* whenever presiding and says the Blessing*.

Procession (Latin – *procedere* – go on, proceed) The proceeding of a body of persons in orderly succession during a religious service or festival. Church processions are often preceded by a crucifer* bearing a processional cross*.

Proper of the Mass (Latin – *proprius* – belonging to) Those parts of the Eucharist* which change according to the festival or season*, as opposed to the Ordinary* of the Mass* (see above).

Proper Preface A passage which comes immediately before the words 'Therefore with angels and archangels and with all the company of heaven' in the Eucharistic* Prayer* and changes according to the festival* or season* to which it gives special emphasis.

Purificator (Latin – *purificare* – to purify) A small cloth used at the Eucharist* to wipe clean the chalice* and paten*.

Pyx (Greek – *puxis* – a box-wood vessel) A small box, often of precious metal, in which the consecrated Host* is kept or carried, especially when taking Communion* to the sick.

Real Presence An expression used in Anglican* Eucharistic* theology* to cover several doctrines* emphasising the actual Presence of the Body and Blood of Christ* in the sacrament*, as contrasted with other views which maintain that the Body and Blood are present only figuratively or symbolically.

Requiem mass (Latin – *requiem* – rest, *requiescat in pace* – *may he/she rest in peace*) A Eucharist* offered for the dead.

Reservation (Latin – *reservere* – to keep) The practice of keeping bread* and wine* consecrated at the Eucharist*. In the earliest days, the faithful often took the sacrament* home from the Sunday Eucharist so that they might receive Communion* during the week. The custom is widely practised today to enable Communion to be taken to the sick as soon as is convenient after the Eucharist has ended, so that priests* are saved from having to celebrate the entire Eucharist for every sick person to whom they, or others, minister the sacrament* at home. The Blessed Sacrament* reserved links the sick person with the Eucharist celebrated in the Parish Church*.

Ritual (Latin – *ritualis*) The prescribed order for performing a religious service (see also **Ceremonial**).

Rubric (Latin – *ruber* – red) The direction, either at the beginning of a service-book or in the course of the text, for the proper ordering of a service or services. In medieval times rubrics were printed in red hence the derivation from the Latin word *ruber*.

Sacristan (Latin – *sacer* – holy) *Either* the sexton* *or*, more commonly, the person or official who has charge of the contents of a church, particularly the vessels and vestments* of the Eucharist*.

Sanctus bell (Latin – *sacer* – holy) also Sacring bell. A small bell rung at the Eucharist* to focus the attention of the people, especially at the Elevation* of the elements*.

Sermon (Latin – *sermo* – speech) Also Address. An extempore or written talk delivered from the pulpit* or elsewhere in a church after the Gospel* at the Eucharist*, and also at other services. Its chief purpose is to proclaim the Gospel* by way of explanation, instruction or exhortation.

Server (Latin – *servire* – to serve) A person (or persons) who assists the celebrant* at the Eucharist* by moving the altar book*, helping with the Offertory*, carrying out the lavabo* and ablutions* and, where provided, ringing the Sanctus bell*.

Species (Latin – *specere* – to look at) The bread* and wine* of the Eucharist*, when consecrated.

Sub-Deacon (see **Deacon**) The minister who assists the Priest* and Deacon* to celebrate the Eucharist*, whose functions are to prepare the bread* and wine* and the vessels, to read or chant the Epistle*, to present the chalice* and paten* at the Offertory*, to pour water into the chalice at the Offertory, and to remove the vessels from the altar* after the Communion*.

Taperer A person who carries a taper (a long wick coated with wax) at the Eucharist*, or at other services, for the lighting of candles.

Thanksgiving The taking of the bread* and cup and the giving of thanks at the Eucharist*, otherwise known as the Eucharistic Prayer or Canon of the Mass*. It follows the Preparation of the Table (Offertory*) (C.W.*)

Thurible (Latin – *thus* – incense) (see **Censer**) A metal vessel for the ceremonial burning of incense* at the Eucharist*. It is usually suspended on chains to allow it to be swung during censing.

Thurifer (see **Thurible**) The person who carries the censer* (thurible*) at the Eucharist*.

Unleavened bread Bread without yeast which is the bread commonly used at the Eucharist*. Jesus Christ used the unleavened bread of the Passover* at the Last Supper. (see Section 8: **Maundy Thursday**, also **Wafer** and **Wine**)

Veil (Latin – *velum* – veil) A square cloth, often embroidered, used to cover the chalice* at the Eucharist*. It can agree with the liturgical colour* of the season* or day (see **Burse**). Veils can also be used to cover other objects. In some churches all crucifixes*, statues and pictures are veiled during Passiontide. (see Section 8: **Lent 5**)

Viaticum (Latin – *viaticus* – provision for a journey) *Either* the Holy Communion* given to those who are likely to die to strengthen them with grace* for their journey into eternity *or* the vessel which contains Holy Communion for the sick.

Vigil (Latin – *vigilans* – awake) A service or prayer* at night (deriving from the ancient widespread belief that the Second Coming of Christ (see **Parousia**) would take place at midnight) used before certain festivals.

Wafer/Host The small disc, usually of unleavened bread*, which is consecrated at the Eucharist* and received by the people at Communion*.

Water The pouring of water into the wine* at the Eucharist* is seen as *either* the common practice in New Testament* times of mingling wine at table with water *or* symbolically as a reminder of the water brought forth from the side of Jesus Christ when he was pierced by a spear at his Crucifixion*.

Wine (Latin – *vinum* – wine) The fermented juice of the grape used by our Lord at the Last Supper, (see Section 8: **Maundy Thursday**) and consecrated* with the bread* at the Eucharist* to become sacramentally* the Body and Blood of Christ.

10 Other Services

1 Sacraments

The two dominical* Sacraments are Holy Baptism* and the Eucharist*. There are five Lesser Sacraments – Confirmation*, Ordination*, Marriage*, Anointing with oil* (Extreme Unction) and Sacramental Confession* (i.e. confession before a bishop* or a priest*). (see Dictionary section for **Sacrament**, see Section 9 for **Eucharist**)

(a) **Holy Baptism** (Latin – *sacer* – holy, *baptisare* – to wash, bathe or immerse) Holy Baptism is the rite by which a person is admitted to the Christian Church*. It is carried out by washing with water* and in the name of the Trinity* – Father, Son and Holy Spirit. It must be preceded by faith* and repentance*. The gifts bestowed by God's grace* in Baptism are union with Christ (through which the believer participates in the victory of his Cross* and Resurrection*), cleansing from sin*, being made a member of the Body of Christ, the Church*, and receiving the gift of the Holy Spirit*. The norm would be baptism when a person is able to understand the meaning, the importance and implications of the sacrament, but infants may be baptised, their parents, god-parents or sponsors making the baptismal promises on their behalf. A god-parent is one who is asked to present a child for baptism and promises to continue to support him or her. A sponsor is one who agrees to support in the journey of faith a candidate of any age for baptism, confirmation or affirmation of baptismal faith*. The BCP* has Baptism services for children and for 'those of riper years', together with a thanksgiving service after the birth of a child. '(Churching of Women*). The C.W.* *Initiation Services* allow several variations e.g. Holy Baptism (the norm), Baptism outside the Eucharist*, Baptism of Children at the Eucharist or at a Service of the Word*, Emergency Baptism, Baptism and Confirmation* (see below) either at or outside the Eucharist, Confirmation at or outside the Eucharist, Affirmation of Baptismal Faith* and Reception* into the Communion* of the Church of England*.

(b) **Confirmation** (Latin – *confirmare* – to make firm) Confirmation is the rite by which a person, having been baptised* and made the baptismal vows, receives, through the laying on of the bishop's* hands, the particular grace* of the Holy Spirit* required to undertake full communicant* membership of the Church*. When a person has been baptised in infancy, the baptismal vows made on that person's behalf by parents, god-parents or sponsors are re-made by the candidate at Confirmation.

(c)   **Ordination** (Latin – *ordo* – order) The forms of service for the ordination of bishops*, priests* and deacons* are to be found in the Ordinal*
of both the BCP* and C.W.* (see Section 3: **Orders**). Ordination is
the rite by which candidates, after due examination, receive, through
the laying on of the bishop's hands, the particular grace* of the Holy
Spirit* required to undertake the responsibilities of the order* to which
they are called.'

(d)   **Marriage** (Latin – *maritus* – of marriage) or Matrimony (Latin –
matrimonium) 'The Church of England* affirms, according to our Lord's
teaching, that marriage is in its nature a union permanent and life-long,
for better for worse, till death them do part, of one man with one
woman, to the exclusion of all others on either side, for the procreation
and nurture of children, for the hallowing and right direction of the
natural instincts and affections, and for the mutual society, help and
comfort which the one ought to have of the other, both in prosperity
and adversity' (Canon* B/30/1 – see Section 2 [3]). Marriage is the
form of service which gives effect to the contents of this Canon. It
should be noted that the bridegroom and bride themselves are the
ministers of the sacrament* of Matrimony. For a marriage to take place
in the Church of England, both parties must be over the age of 16, one
of them must be baptised* and they must not be related to each other
in one of the prohibited degrees of affinity*, e.g. a man may not marry
his sister. Before a marriage is solemnised, certain legal formalities to
ensure there are no objections to the marriage and to prove residence
or waive residence, have to be completed. These are known as Banns
of Marriage (21 days' residence) (Teutonic – *bann* – proclamation with
penalties), or, alternatively, a Superintendent Registrar's Certificate of
Banns, or a Common Licence (15 days' residence) which entails the
swearing of an affidavit before a surrogate* and the issuing of a licence
by the Diocesan Registrar*, or an Archbishop's* Licence (residence
not required) which entails application to and issue of licence by the
Archbishop of Canterbury's Legal Registrar.

As far as the marriage in church* of a person who is divorced and has
a partner still living is concerned, there are two divergent possibilities
open. According to the Rules of Convocation*, a member of the clergy*
may not marry in church a person in this category. Many clergy who
follow these Rules offer instead a service of prayer*, dedication and blessing following upon a marriage ceremony held in a civil register office (see
Section 13, subsection 4). But the law of the land i.e. civil law, does permit
a member of the clergy to marry in church a person in this category and
many now do exercise this right. The decision as to which possibility to
use rests entirely with the member of the clergy concerned. (In the C.W.*
series, the Marriage service appears in *Pastoral Services*.)

(e)   **Anointing**
There are three distinct uses of oil in the life of the Church*
    (i) the oil used to anoint the sick*, following the example of the
        apostles* and the teaching of St James*.

(ii) the oil used as part of the preparation for Baptism*, sometimes called the oil of catechumens*.

(iii) the oil of chrism, (Greek – *khrio* – anoint) the use of which symbolises the anointing by the Holy Spirit of monarchs, and of those who are baptised, confirmed* or ordained*. Chrism may also be used to set apart objects for religious purposes, e.g. altars*, churches, sacred vessels, etc. Whereas the first and second oils are usually olive oil, the oil of chrism is a mixture of olive oil and balsam.

The anointing of the sick with oil is sometimes called Extreme Unction (Latin – *extremus* – outermost – *unctio* – anointing). The name Extreme Unction originally designated the unction which a Christian* received last, i.e. after the anointing in Baptism and the anointing in Confirmation (see (iii) above), but not necessarily at the point of death (*in extremis*), though the sacrament* was frequently administered in this situation. The scope of this rite* has been broadened in recent times. It may now be administered to all who are seriously ill, and more than once during the same illness if a new crisis arises.

The three kinds of oils are usually blessed by bishops* in their cathedrals* on Maundy Thursday*, but, in cases of necessity, e.g. in times of acute sickness, the priest* administering the sacrament may bless the oil. Anointing of the sick with oil is now an authorised alternative service in the Church of England*. (See Wholeness and Healing in the C.W.* series *Pastoral Services*)

(f) **Sacramental Confession** (or Auricular Confession – Latin – *ad auriculum* – to the ear, i.e. of a bishop* or priest*) Confession of sins* to God by an individual in the presence of a bishop* or priest. The rite* requires repentance* and an intention to try to mould one's life more closely to the pattern of Christ. After examination and counsel by the bishop or priest, the bishop or priest is authorised to forgive* the individual in God's Name. Although there is no rite in the BCP*, in the first Exhortation contained in the Communion* service, encourages those who are unable to quieten their consciences to seek spiritual counsel and absolution* from a priest. There is a form of absolution in the Order for the Visitation of the Sick in the BCP. The practice is not universal in the Church of England, more emphasis being placed on the public confession of sin, but a rite is provided in the C.W.* series *Initiation Services*.

Other Offices

(a) **Daily Offices** (Latin – *officium* – from *facere* – to do) The daily authorised public prayer* of the Church* which the clergy* have a special obligation to recite.

(i) **Divine Service** (Latin – *servitium divinum*) A title reserved for the choir offices* of the Church's worship* i.e. Morning and Evening Prayer*.

(ii) **Morning Prayer** (also known as Mattins (French – *matin* – morning)) Originally an office* recited in the middle of the night, and taking its structure from that office, with additions from the ancient office of Prime. C.W.* allows much more flexibility in its use, e.g. if it is recited before the Eucharist*, parts of it may be omitted.

(iii) **Evening Prayer** (also known as Evensong) A conflation of the offices* of Vespers and Compline* in the ancient Sarum (Salisbury) Rite*. Like Morning Prayer, it is based on the recitation of the Psalms*, readings from the Old and New Testaments*, canticles* and prayers.

(iv) **Compline** (Latin – *completus* – completed) The last office* of the day which completes the daily round of prayer. The recitation of this office is not obligatory, but is widely used. (It is also known as Night Prayer.)

(b)   **Occasional Offices**

(i) **Ministry to the Sick**

C.W.* in *Pastoral Services*, Wholeness and Healing, provides a range of services for use with the sick, i.e. Communion* with the Sick, the Laying on of Hands* with Prayer*, Anointing*, and prayers.

(ii) **Funeral** (Latin – *funus* – funeral)

Burial* of a corpse in a coffin in a grave is the traditional Christian method of disposing of the dead, but, in recent times, cremation, i.e. the reducing of a body to ashes by burning, has become widely accepted as an alternative. Cremation takes place in a crematorium. Forms of service are prescribed in both BCP* and C.W.*, but C.W., in Pastoral Services, Funerals and Ministry at the Time of Death, has made provision for services to be used on other occasions surrounding a death e.g. at the interment (burial) of ashes and at the funeral of a child. A service of Holy Communion* may also be incorporated in a funeral service (see **Requiem Mass**).

(iii) **Litany** (Greek – *litaneia* – prayer)

A series of petitions* for use in church services or processions*, recited or sung by a member of the clergy* or cantor*, and responded to, usually in repeated phrases, by the people. It is used at Ordination*, often during Advent* and Lent*, and, in some places, on Fridays (see also Section 8: **Easter 5**).

(iv) **Churching of Women** A form of thanksgiving after childbirth BCP*. It is based on the Jewish rite* of purification. The service is not now widely used in the Church of England.

(c)   **Other services**

(i) **The Three Hours' Devotion**

A service held on Good Friday* during the three hours of our Lord's Passion* from noon to 3 o'clock. It often consists of sermons* on the Seven 'Words' spoken by our Lord from the Cross*, with hymns* and prayers interspersed, but, in recent times, there has been much more flexibility in its construction.

(ii) **Benediction** (see Section 9)

11 Creeds

The word 'creed' derives from the Latin word *credo* – I believe. It is a brief, formal and authorised summary of the Christian faith*. In the earliest days creeds were very short indeed, e.g. 'I believe Jesus is Lord' or 'I believe Jesus is the Son of God', but, as a result of the heresies (the denial or doubting of specific articles of faith) of the early centuries, longer statements became necessary.

1   **The Apostles' Creed** (used at Morning and Evening Prayer*) It is the first of the longer creeds to emerge. It is a product of the *Western* Church. It is very terse and does not go into theological* detail. It is very unlikely that it was composed by the Apostles* or their successors, but an abbreviated form of it was probably in use at Rome as early as A.D.* 150. By A.D. 390, a slightly shorter version of this Creed was widely used in the West, and, by the eighth century, it had taken on its present shape.

2   **The Nicene Creed** (used at the Eucharist* and at Ordination*) Strictly speaking, there are two Nicene Creeds. The earlier of the two was formulated at the Council of Nicea in A.D. 325, from whence it derives its name. It was drawn up by the Council to defend the faith against the attacks of the Arian heresy* (Christ not divine, but created by the Father). This creed was relatively short. It is thought possible that the Council of Constantinople in A.D. 381 took parts of the Nicene Creed and greatly expanded it to its present form. Wherever it came from, the Creed, as we know it today, was based on the Baptismal Creed of Jerusalem. It is therefore a product of the *Eastern* Church.

3   **The Athanasian Creed** (rarely used, but appears in the BCP* after Morning Prayer* under the heading 'At Morning Prayer', its subtitle being *Quicunque Vult*, the Latin words for 'Whosoever will', the first words of the Creed). It was not composed by St Athanasius because it deals with heresies* which did not arise until after his death. It is a product of the *Western* Church and emerged, in Latin, from Gaul between A.D. 381 and 428. It was written to refute the heresy of Apollinarianism (Christ fully divine, but not fully human) and is a detailed exposition of the Trinity*.

12 The Bible

The Bible is the story of God's covenant* with his people, first with the Jews, as revealed in the Old Testament*, and then with the whole of the human race, as revealed in the New, through the salvation* won by the death and resurrection* of his Son Jesus Christ*. Many Bibles also contain the Apocrypha*.

The intention in this section is to list the books and documents of the Old and New Testaments, giving, in most cases, a brief description of type and contents, indicating the approximate date of their appearance, and the approximate date of the period in history in which they are set.

Old Testament

BEGINNINGS

The Pentateuch (Greek – *penta* – five, *teukhos* – book) The first five books of the Old Testament – Genesis*, Exodus*, Leviticus*, Numbers*, Deuteronomy*. Although they are attributed to Moses, most Biblical* scholars agree that they are compilations of previously written, no longer existing, documents dating from the ninth to the fifth centuries B.C.* These documents are generally denoted by letters – 'J' (see **Yahweh**), 'E' (see **Elohim**), 'D' (Deuteronomy*) and also 'P' – the Priestly source, i.e. those documents which are marked by an emphasis on ritual* and ceremonial* details as opposed to narrative (e.g. Exodus 25–40, Leviticus and much of Numbers). Extracts from different documents can be found in different books of the Pentateuch. Approximate date of the first appearance of each source document:

J   circa   900 B.C.
E   circa   800 B.C.————Pentateuch completed in its present form
D   emerged   621 B.C.————by circa 370 B.C.
P   circa   450 B.C.

Genesis (Greek – *gen* – become) (The Hebrew title of this book is *Bereshith* which means 'in the beginning', the first words of the book) The earlier part of the book contains the stories which the writers of long ago used to explain in their own way the truths and realities of which they were aware, e.g. the Creation, the Fall*, the Flood. The later part of the book records the lives of the great Patriarchs (Fathers) of the Jewish race – Abraham, Isaac, Jacob, Joseph. For the Christian, Genesis contains the Biblical* basis for much Christian doctrine* – the Creation, the Fall and

the idea of Covenant*. For the date the book appeared see Pentateuch*.
Period of history – pre-history to c. 1550 B.C.

Exodus (Greek – *exodos* – way out) This book records the events surrounding
what for the Jewish world has remained the outstanding instance of
the showing of God's favour to his chosen people, i.e. the release of
the Israelites under Moses from their slavery in Egypt and their journey-
ings in the wilderness towards the Promised Land of Canaan. The
symbolism of the Passover* and God's act of rescue was used by the
early Christian community to describe the work of Christ, whose own
death took place at the Feast of the Passover (see also Section 8: Introduction, Section 9: **Paschal candle**, Section 14: **Paschal lamb**). The
book also provides social laws and deals with matters of priestly ceremonial.
For the date the book appeared see Pentateuch*
Period of history – c. 1290–1250 B.C.

Leviticus The name is derived from Levi who was regarded as the father of
the Hebrew priesthood. The whole book is concerned with priestly
laws – about sacrifice, the consecration of priests, ritual purity, priests'
dues. It also describes the Day of Atonement* and contains the Holiness
Code.
For the date the book appeared see Pentateuch*
Period of history – a gathering of laws from before the time of Moses
c. 1300 B.C. to long after the settlement in Canaan c. 1200 B.C.

Numbers Lists and genealogies, i.e. 'family trees', laws, wilderness wanderings
and conflicts east of Jordan. For the date the book appeared see Pentateuch*
Period of history – c. 1290–1250 B.C.

Deuteronomy (Greek – *deutero* – second, *nomos* – law) A copy of the Law.
This is a much later book than the other four. It is thought that the
Book of the Law which was found in the Temple at Jerusalem, and
was the basis of King Josiah's Reformation in 621 B.C., was, in fact,
the central section of Deuteronomy.
    Exhortations and a code of laws based on beliefs in the special
relationship of Israel with God, in the one sanctuary (i.e. the Temple),
in the law of justice, rewards and punishments and in the need for
humanitarian attitudes.
For the date the book appeared see Pentateuch*
Period of history – c. 650 B.C.

HISTORY

Joshua After the death of Moses, Joshua took over as leader of the Israelites and
crossed into Canaan. Jericho and Ai captured. The Gibeonite coalition
defeated. The Canaanite coalition defeated. The conquest completed,
Canaan was divided among the tribes. Death of Joshua.
Several sources edited by c. 620 B.C.
Period of history – c. 1250–1200 B.C.

Judges History is used to illustrate and reveal the character and work of Israel's God. The book contains an account of twelve judges (rulers or leaders), including Deborah, Gideon, Jephthah and Samson. The teaching is prophetic – Israel goes after other gods – God sends a foreign enemy to punish her – Israel repents and God sends a leader to deliver her. A sanctuary is founded at Dan – the men of Benjamin are punished.

Several sources edited by c. 620 B.C.

Period of history – c. 1200–1020 B.C.

Ruth It is not an historical book, but derives its position in the Old Testament from the placing of the story in the time of the Judges. It is a charming love story with a lesson to teach – that God's people need to be reminded that his revelation of himself to them brings both privilege and responsibility; this revelation must be kept unpolluted and be available to all.

Suggested date for the appearance of the book – c. 425 B.C.

Period of history – c. 1200–1020 B.C.

1 Samuel The story of Samuel, prophet, priest and seer, and his call by God. The foundation of the monarchy – Saul anointed by Samuel and proclaimed first King. Relationships between Samuel and Saul. The story of Saul, David and Jonathan. David is outlawed – spares Saul's life twice. Saul perishes at Gilboa.

Several sources edited – c. 620 B.C.

Period of history – c. 1020–1000 B.C.

2 Samuel David reigns as King in Judah for seven years before becoming King of the united Kingdom of Judah (south) and Israel (north). Jerusalem becomes the capital city and the Ark is taken there. A temple is planned and God's favour is promised to David's line. Court intrigues and attempts to overthrow David.

Several sources edited – c. 620 B.C.

Period of history – c. 1000–961 B.C.

1 Kings The death of David. Solomon establishes himself on the throne. Solomon's reign and wisdom. The building and dedication of the Temple. Solomon's wealth and influence. Solomon's sin – his peoples rebel. Revolt of the northern tribes; the kingdom divides on the death of Solomon (c. 922 B.C.) Elijah the prophet battles to preserve the life of Israel against foreign cults and customs. Miracle stories. Elisha called. Elijah in conflict with King Ahab and Jezebel – Naboth's vineyard.

Several sources edited – c. 620 B.C.

Period of history – c. 961–850 B.C.

2 Kings The last days of Elijah. Elisha succeeds him. More miracles. Jehu's revolution. Accounts of the lives of the Kings of Judah and Israel down to the fall of Samaria (c. 722 B.C.). Account of the history of Judah: discovery of a law-book (Deuteronomy*) during repair work on the Temple. King Josiah's reform based on this book (621 B.C.). More history of Judah to the fall of Jerusalem – the destruction of the Temple (587 B.C.) and the departure of the Jews into exile in Babylon.

Several sources edited – from c. 620 B.C.

Period of history – c. 850–570 B.C.

1 Chronicles Originally the two books of the Chronicles and the books of Ezra* and Nehemiah* formed one book. Much influencing from the Deuteronomic* and Priestly (see **Pentateuch**) schools. The Chronicler is interested in the holy community (established by God and maintained by him through all the trials of history) and its worship centred on the Temple in Jerusalem.

Genealogies – the tribes of Israel and Judah. The history of David. The accession of Solomon.

Suggested date for the appearance of the book – c. 350 B.C.

Period of history – c. 1000–961 B.C.

2 Chronicles The reign of Solomon. The history of the Kings of Judah to the captivity.

Suggested date for the appearance of the book – c. 350 B.C.

Period of history – c. 961–570 B.C.

(the Exile 587–538 B.C.)

Ezra Originally united with Nehemiah. Ezra was a scribe who went to Jerusalem with a party of exiles returning rather later than most. The book is in two parts, separated by a gap of possibly more than half a century. The first part gives an account of the return of the captives from Babylon at the beginning of the reign of Cyrus (538 B.C.), and the rebuilding of the Temple, which was interrupted by the Samaritans but completed in 516 B.C. in the reign of Darius. In the second part, an account is given of the second return of exiles in the reign of Artaxerxes in 457 B.C.

Suggested date for the appearance of the book – c. 350 B.C.

Period of history – 538–457 B.C.

Nehemiah Nehemiah, cupbearer to the King of Persia, heard of the plight of Jerusalem and the people of Judea. Artaxerxes commissioned him to rebuild the walls of the city, a task he completed in fifty-two days in spite of much opposition. He was later instrumental in putting an end to many of the abuses he found in Jerusalem.

Suggested date for the appearance of the book – c. 350 B.C.

Period of history – c. 445–432 B.C.

Esther A fictional episode in the history of those Israelites who did not return from the Captivity. Esther, a Jewess, Mordecai's adopted daughter, becomes the King's favourite wife. Haman plots to destroy the Jewish exiles. Mordecai discovers this and tells Esther, who takes her life in her hands and pleads with the King for her people. Haman is hanged, Mordecai is promoted and the Jews slaughter their enemies.

Suggested date for the appearance of the book – c. 250 B.C.

Period of history-c. 480 B.C.

POETRY

Job A classic statement of the problem of human suffering. Why do those who are righteous have to suffer so much pain and misery, when those who are wicked so often seem to prosper? The major part of the book is a dialogue between the righteous Job who has to endure many hardships and his three so-called friends, Eliphaz, Bildad and Zophar. God intervenes eventually in a passage revealing his power and wisdom. Job realises his error in questioning God's ways, turns back to him and is duly rewarded.

Suggested date for the appearance of the book – c. 400 B.C. It has no historical basis.

Psalms It is often called the hymn* book of the Second Temple (post 510 B.C.) because it was widely used in its liturgy*. It is the bringing together of a number of collections of psalms, written by different people at different times. There are hymns of praise to God, the Lord of nature, of history, and of his chosen people, expressions of national and personal sorrow, personal prayers and thanksgivings, communings with God, songs in praise of wisdom, and psalms for special occasions – royal hymns, prophetic songs and a small number of cursing psalms. It is unlikely that David himself was responsible for more than a very small number of psalms.

The collection, as we have it today, may have been completed by c. 200 B.C..

Proverbs An anthology of wise sayings, both from Israel and elsewhere, which enshrines much profound thought about human conditions. Just as the Psalms in their entirety were wrongly attributed to David, so the Proverbs were in the same way wrongly attributed to Solomon. The wise are those who systematically dedicate themselves to the discovery of the way of God; those who follow his laws will enjoy long life and prosperity.

The collection may have been completed by c. 300 B.C.

Ecclesiastes Probably written in Jerusalem, the book is fatalistic in its thinking. Man's freedom is limited. The author is obsessed by the emptiness of life and the inevitability of death.

Suggested date for the appearance of the book – c. 250 B.C.

Song of Solomon A song, or a collection of songs, in praise of the beauties of the natural world and the wonder and mystery of human love. Probably written in the north, rather than in Judaea.

Suggested date for the appearance of the book – c. 300 B.C.

PROPHECY

Isaiah:First Isaiah (Isaiah chapters 1–39) The prophet of First Isaiah was called by God in the year of King Uzziah's death (c. 740 B.C.). He spent his whole life in Jerusalem and was probably a member of the court. He was active as a prophet during the reigns of Jotham and Ahaz and most of that of Hezekiah. During his active years, he gathered a band of disciples around him who preserved his sayings and added to them. Isaiah came on the scene at a time of grave crisis for the nation. Assyria had conquered the north and dominated Judah in the south. Greed, corruption and poverty walked side by side. The nation's religion had become a ritual sham. Isaiah compared the holiness of God with the depravity of the nation's wickedness. But there would be some who would remain faithful to God – a faithful remnant – repenting of their sins and trusting in God's promises. And, one day, a King of David's line – a Messiah* – would come to restore God's universal reign. So the future hope of Israel was born. The collecting together of the prophecies covers a long period, possibly from 600 to 450 B.C.

Period of history – c. 740–700 B.C.

Second Isaiah (Isaiah chapters 40–55) The author is unknown, but was a contemporary of King Cyrus. He conveys a message of comfort. After the destruction of Jerusalem, a time of restoration is at hand. There will be a new Jerusalem where God will demonstrate his sovereignty over other gods by his wisdom and providence. And he will be a God for all the peoples. This part of Isaiah contains the four Songs of the Suffering Servant. The servant of God redeems his people from their sins by his own death and is exalted by God to a position of glory. Not unnaturally, he has been seen by many as foreshadowing Christ.

The chapters emerged possibly c. 450 B.C.

Period of history – c. 540 B.C.

Third Isaiah (Isaiah chapters 56–66) A collection of prophecies from several sources, probably deriving from Second Isaiah's disciples. The chapters emerged possibly c. 450 B.C.

Period of history – c. 540–489 B.C.

Jeremiah Jeremiah was born in about 645 B.C. of a priestly family living near Jerusalem. God called him in the thirteenth year of King Josiah's reign (c. 627 B.C.). He was to live through turbulent times, culminating in the rise to power of Nebuchadnezzar, King of Babylon, who captured Jerusalem in 597 B.C., after a rebellion by Judah, and deported some of its inhabitants. A further rebellion by Judah led to the destruction of Jerusalem and the burning of the Temple in 587 B.C. More inhabitants were deported into exile. Jeremiah prophesied disaster, constantly admonished the Judean Kings and was branded a defeatist. He was persecuted and thrown into prison. When Jerusalem fell, he chose to stay in Palestine with the governor Gedaliah, but, when Gedaliah was murdered, he was taken to Egypt by a group of fleeing Jews.

Jeremiah was a man of peace – a gentle man – whose lot was to be involved in strife and dissension. He saw it as his duty, laid upon him by God, to continue to prophesy against all that was false in the life of his nation, even though it meant his own suffering. But, out of his suffering, there developed a friendship with God – a confidence and trust that God can be known on a personal level. So he could speak of a new covenant – a covenant written in the heart. The book is a compilation from several sources and may not have appeared in its present form until c. 500 B.C. or much later.

Period of history – c. 627–587 B.C..

Lamentations Most scholars agree that it is unlikely that Jeremiah is the author – several statements contradict his thinking. The book consists of five poems. Out of the mourning for the fallen city of Jerusalem, there emerges an unquenchable trust in God.

Suggested date for the book's appearance – c. 540 B.C..

Period of history – 587–580 B.C..

Ezekiel It is thought that Ezekiel was actively preaching in Palestine until the fall of Jerusalem in 587 B.C.., after which he continued his ministry amongst the exiles in Babylon. Ezekiel was a priest for whom the Temple was the over-riding interest – the destroyed Temple from which God's glory had departed, or the Temple of the future to which God would return. He upholds the priority of the Law. He uses symbolic pictures to drive home his message – the four living creatures of the Lord's chariot and the valley of the dry bones are particularly vivid. Ezekiel's teaching is based on the need for inner conversion to the ways of God, a conversion which will bring from God a 'new heart and a new spirit'.

Suggested date for the emergence of the book – c. 450 B.C..

Period of history – c. 597–571 B.C..

Daniel Not a truly prophetic book. It was written by someone who wished to conceal his identity because of the fear of persecution. The persecution was probably that of Antiochus IV Epiphanes who reigned from 175–163 B.C.., particularly remembered for his desecration of the Temple in 168 B.C.. ('the abomination of desolation'). The book aims to strengthen the faith of the suffering Jews. It falls into two parts. The first six chapters are stories of the way in which Daniel and his companions triumphed over the trials they had to endure, (e.g. the fiery furnace, the lions' den) obliging their persecutors to acknowledge the power and sovereignty of God. The last six chapters are visions, in which the destruction of the persecutor and the end are foretold. God's Kingdom will come, ruled over by one like a son of man. Daniel is the prime example of Old Testament apocalyptic* literature.

Suggested date for the appearance of the book – c. 165 B.C.

Period of history 168–165 B.C.

Hosea Hosea lived in the northern Kingdom of Israel. A baker by trade, Hosea's marriage to Gomer became for him an allegory. Gomer was continually unfaithful – a reflection of Israel's unfaithfulness to God, both in its religious and political life. Hosea uses the ideals of a true marriage relationship to show the people of Israel what God requires of them – righteousness, justice, loyalty, mercy, and all based on a knowledge of God.

Suggested date for the appearance of the book – c. 650 B.C.

Period of history – c. 746–725 B.C.

Joel Joel was probably a prophet attached to the Temple. The book falls into two parts. In the first, the prophet describes an impending invasion of locusts and calls the people to repentance and prayer. The first part is linked to the second by the apocalyptic* concept of the Day of the Lord. The nations will be judged, but the Lord will triumph and will pour out his spirit on all flesh.

Suggested date for the appearance of the book – c. 350 B.C.

Period of history – c. 450 B.C.

Amos Amos was a herdsman from Tekoa in Judah, about twelve miles from Jerusalem. In the reign of Jeroboam II, God called Amos and sent him to Bethel to prophesy against the corruption, injustice, vice and religious prostitution prevalent in his day. He warned his compatriots of the coming Day of the Lord, a Lord who is all-powerful, a universal Lord who demands justice.

Suggested date for the appearance of the book – c. 720 B.C. or later

Period of history c. 755–745 B.C.

Obadiah Much of the book is also found in Jeremiah, but it is difficult to say which was written first. The prophecy has two parts – in the first, Edom is threatened with vengeance for gloating over the discomfiture of Israel at the fall of Jerusalem. The second part threatens a wider retribution when the Day of the Lord comes.

Suggested date for the appearance of the book – c. 500 B.C.

Period of history 586 B.C.

Jonah A fictional prophet. The book teaches that, in God's providence, even those who do not belong to his Chosen People, can offer him both penitence and worship and be accepted by him.

The book appeared possibly – c. 330 B.C.

Micah A prophet in Judah during the reigns of Ahaz and Hezekiah. He is a countryman and very suspicious of his urban compatriots. He sees himself as a messenger of God and is not frightened to prophesy disaster, unlike the false prophets. God puts Israel on trial and finds her people guilty of immorality and corruption. But there will be a brighter future when God will reign again in Zion, and one from Ephrathah will rule. But this will not come until Israel has learned its lesson and turned again to righteousness. Then there will be hope – Israel will be restored and her enemies destroyed.

Suggested date for the appearance of the book – c. 520 B.C.

Period of history – c.730–701 B.C.

Nahum The book is a series of poems rejoicing in the fall of the city of Nineveh to the Babylonians and Medes in 612 B.C. It is God's judgement on those who oppose him. He is the sovereign Lord of history.

Suggested date for the appearance of the book – c. 600 B.C.

Period of history – c. 615–610 B.C.

Habbakuk God makes use of the Chaldeans to punish his people, but they, in their turn, will be punished by God because of their cruelty. God will save his people. Unlike the rest of the prophets, Habbakuk questions God's actions in seemingly allowing evil to triumph. But, even though his ways are hard to understand, his righteousness will, in the end, prevail.

Suggested date for the appearance of the book – c. 597 B.C.

Period of history – c. 605–597 B.C.

Zephaniah The prophet was active during the reign of Josiah. He warns that the Day of the Lord will be a day of punishment for those who ignore his laws. He thunders not only against Judah's corruption, but also against the arrogance of the nations. Obedience and humility are prerequisites to the salvation enjoyed only by a humble remnant.

Suggested date for the appearance of the book – c. 630 B.C.

Period of history – c. 640–630 B.C.

Haggai A contemporary of the prophet Zechariah*; both were active after the Exile. When the exiles returned from Babylon to rebuild the Temple, they soon became disheartened. Haggai and Zechariah put fresh heart into them, and persuaded Zerubbabel the governor and Joshua the high priest to resume working on the Temple. The new Temple's glory would far outshine the glory of the old – and would usher in a new age.

Suggested date for the appearance of the book – c. 519 B.C.

Period of history – 520 B.C.

Zechariah Like Haggai*, Zechariah concentrates on the rebuilding of the Temple, and sees it as a symbol of national restoration and an urgent reminder of the coming of a messianic era in which God's servant 'the Branch' will rule on his behalf – a message transmitted in a series of visions. Whereas the first eight chapters are basically thought to be the work of Zechariah, chapters 9–14 are from a different hand and a different time. They speak of promise – Judah, at present under the heel of a foreign oppressor, will have its own royal saviour. Although its people are down-trodden now, they will, in future, become all-powerful, and Jerusalem will become the religious centre of the world.

Part One of the book (Chapters 1–8) is thought to have appeared c. 519 B.C.

Period of history – 520 B.C.

Part two of the book (Chapters 9–14) is thought to have appeared c. 320 B.C.

Period of history – an apocalyptic* episode based on the rebuilding of the Temple 520 B.C.

Malachi ('My messenger') An anonymous author active long after the Exile. God is a loving father and ruler of his people. They have failed him – priests and people neglect their spiritual duties – mixed marriage and divorce are rife. But the Day of the Lord will be a purifying fire – the Lord's messenger will see to it. It is the righteous who will triumph.

Suggested date for the appearance of the book – c. 460 B.C.

Period of history – c. 470 B.C.

New Testament

The Gospels (Old English – *god spel* – good tidings) The good news about the coming of the Kingdom of God*, proclaimed in word and deed by Jesus Christ, the Son of God.

The Synoptic Gospels The problem of the literary relationships between the Gospels of Matthew*, Mark* and Luke* is known as the Synoptic

(Greek – *sunoptikos* – seen together) Problem, and arises from the occurrence of a large amount of common subject matter and similar phrasing in all three. Part of the problem centres on a document which may have existed but is no longer extant and is given the code letter 'Q'. It is thought to have been the source of those passages in the Gospels of Matthew and Luke which show a close similarity to each other, but not to anything in the Gospel of Mark. There are many other theories about the relationships between the three.

Matthew Matthew's Gospel probably appeared a little after A.D. 70. Many scholars agree that its author is unlikely to have been Matthew, but it was obviously written for a community with strong Jewish connections, since the Old Testament* is used more widely in Matthew than in the other three Gospels.

Mark Many hold that Mark's Gospel was the first to appear. It is dated c. A.D. 65 and was probably written in Rome. The authorship is uncertain, but it is clear that whoever wrote it was either a friend of or knew a friend of Peter, because of the emphasis placed on him in the text. Mark is the shortest of the Gospels – a terse narrative dedicated to giving the important facts of the story.

Luke Luke's Gospel is said to have appeared c. A.D. 80–85, possibly from Achaia. There is general agreement that it was written by Luke himself (the companion of Paul). It was certainly written in and for the Gentile* world, particularly to show that Christ's mission* was universal and not restricted to the Jewish community. Luke lays great emphasis on the work of our Lord amongst the outcasts of his society. Because it is generally agreed that Luke also wrote the Book of the Acts of the

Acts Apostles, his Gospel and Acts taken together provide a comprehensive
Out of account not only of the ministry of Christ, but also of the growth of
sequence the early Church*.

John The dating and authorship of John's Gospel are obscure. Tradition places the writing of the Gospel in Ephesus, and a date c. A.D. 100 is generally accepted. John is related to three worlds of thought – the primitive Christian tradition about Jesus – Judaism (Jewish – based) – and Hellenistic (Greek – based) thought (see the Prologue to John 1.1– 18 and Dictionary section: **Logos**). The Gospel is more meditative than the other three, and is not concerned to maintain their same order of events. Many of the passages ascribed to Jesus are probably the author's own interpretation and development of our Lord's teaching. The Gospel proclaims that Jesus is the Messiah* and Son of God and its teaching, based on the 'signs' that Jesus gave of his glory*, is aimed to bring the reader to believe in him as Messiah and so to have life and have it more abundantly.

The Epistles (Latin – *epistola* – letter) The Letters of Paul, the Pastoral Letters, the Letter to the Hebrews (i.e. Jewish Christians), the Letters of James, Peter, John and Jude.

Paul's Letters Paul was the first great missionary* and teacher of the Church. Paul's missionary strategy followed a consistent pattern throughout his three extended journeys. He would visit a centre, establish a Christian community, staying with them for a long or short period, and then move on, having appointed leaders. He kept in touch with the communities, either by writing letters to them or by re-visiting them or both. He also answered by letter the problems they brought to his notice.

Romans c. A.D. 57 (from Corinth) Both Jew and Gentile* alike are in need of the good news of the Gospel*. Paul outlines God's new plan of salvation* – we are justified by faith* through God's grace*. For those who are in Christ, there is new life in the freedom of the Spirit* – a new life not possible for those who stick slavishly to the Law.

Paul gives practical advice about the duties of a Christian as citizen and compassionate neighbour.

1 Corinthians c. A.D. 54 (from Ephesus) Paul attacks those who have sought to divide the Christian community and questioned his authority as an apostle*. He condemns the cases of immorality which have been reported and gives directions about meat sacrificed to idols. The multiplicity of spiritual gifts, and their proper use, are basic to the life of the Church*. But the climax of his message is the Christian hope of resurrection*.

2 Corinthians 1–9 c. A.D. 56 (from Macedonia) Paul speaks in his own defence. He is a minister of a new covenant* and a preacher of the Gospel through which the glory* of Christ is revealed. He appeals for reconciliation* and asks for a generous response to the collection for the Christians in Jerusalem.

2 Corinthians 10–13 c. A.D. 55 (from Ephesus) Paul defends himself. His authority remains, even though he may have given cause for criticism. His record of suffering for Christ is second to none. He is prepared to be very firm with the trouble makers.

Galatians c. A.D. 56 (? from Macedonia) Paul speaks of his conversion* and the authenticity of his apostleship. He compares his mission to the Gentiles with Peter's mission to the Jews – both recognised as valid, as witnessed by the friendly conclusion of the meeting in Jerusalem. He warns the Galatians against putting the Law before faith* in Christ and calls for a recognition of the fruits of the Spirit* as the foundation of the Christian life.

Ephesians c. A.D. 60 (from Rome) Paul proclaims the mystery of the Gospel and reminds his readers of their privileged place in God's purposes. He has been sent by God to share this mystery* with the Gentiles. He exhorts the Ephesians to live in unity* with each other in Christ, to uphold high standards, particularly in the home. They have the whole armour of God to defend them against the onslaughts of an evil world.

Philippians c. A.D. 56 (from Ephesus) Paul thanks the Philippians for their friendship, for their steadfastness in the faith and for their gifts. They must stand firm and be united in love, remembering always how Christ won salvation* for them. He warns against those who think salvation lies in the Law, and calls for constant efforts to reflect the mind of Christ in behaviour and relationships.

Colossians c. A.D. 60 (from Rome) All the fullness of God rests in Christ, and the Christians at Colossae have their share in his salvation*. But Paul warns them not to be misled by the theories of those who speculate about the cosmos. Their union with Christ gives them all the encouragement they need to live lives full of his love* and peace.

1 Thessalonians c. A.D. 50 (from Corinth) Paul defends his behaviour toward the Christians in Thessalonika and thanks God for their faith and patience. He encourages them to live and work in such a way that they earn the respect of those amongst whom they live. He calms their fears about the fate of the dead and speaks of the Day of the Lord – the Parousia* – the return of Christ to claim his Kingdom, which Paul believed, at that time, to be imminent.

2 Thessalonians c. A.D. 51 (from Corinth) Paul gives thanks for their faith* and endurance. He says more about the coming of the Lord, but seems to indicate it may not happen as soon as he had previously thought. So they need to stand firm in their faith, distancing themselves from those who disrupt their unity* or do not pull their weight.

Philemon c. A.D. 60 (from Rome) Paul tells Philemon, one of his converts, *Out of* that Onesimus, Philemon's slave and also a convert of Paul, has returned *sequence* after running away. He pleads for compassionate treatment and, although he accepts that Philemon still owns Onesimus, he encourages them to live as brothers with the same Master.

The Pastoral Letters Their authorship is uncertain and there is much to suggest they were not written by Paul. This makes their dating very difficult.

1 Timothy Warnings against false teachers. The purpose of the Law. Instructions about prayer*, women, elders, deacons*, widows and slaves.

2 Timothy Timothy is reminded of the gifts he has received from God and is exhorted to stand firm in spite of the difficulties he has to face. He is warned to be on his guard against false teachers and encouraged to live an upright life. The last days will bring many hardships, but Timothy must continue to proclaim the Gospel* with steadfast faith*.

Titus What is expected in elders. False teachers condemned. The behaviour of the Christian as a response to the example of Christ's sacrifice.

The Letter to the Hebrews, possibly c. A.D.68. The internal evidence in the letter indicates almost certainly that it was not written by Paul. Its argument is based entirely on the Old Testament*. God has often spoken before, but Christ, his Son, the heir, the Lord of creation is his final word. He has achieved what no other could – the salvation* of the human race. He is therefore greater than the angels*, than Moses or Joshua. His priesthood is greater than, different to the ancient priesthood of the Hebrews. His is a new covenant* sealed with his own blood. His sacrifice* is greater than any demanded by the Law.

So, with Christ's supremacy before them, those who follow him must be faithful to him, learn from the examples of God's great servants of the past, be ready to accept hardship, and remain faithful to the One who is the same yesterday, today and for ever.

James possibly c. A.D. 100. The author is unknown. The letter is addressed to the twelve tribes of the Dispersion, i.e. to the Jewish Christians scattered all over the Greco-Roman world. It presumes its readers are familiar with the Old Testament*, especially with its Wisdom literature. It is a long list of instructions on how the Christian should behave and act. Those who ignore Christian standards are condemned. All must be patient in hardship. Those who are sick should seek anointing* and the prayers* of the Church*.

1 Peter possibly pre A.D. 67, or later. (from Rome) It is thought that the letter may have been the work of the Apostle* himself or the work of an amanuensis writing later on Peter's instructions and authority A valuable summary of the theology* of the apostles*. Christians must suffer patiently, like Christ, when their faith* results in hardship and persecution. They must be good citizens, servants, wives and husbands – old and young alike must display the Christian virtues.

2 Peter possibly c. A.D. 90. The authorship is uncertain. The author expects the believer to respond with high standards of behaviour to the generosity of God's promises who allows us to share in the divine nature. It warns against false teachers and the punishment to come for those who are morally corrupt. The Day of the Lord will come, even though there may be delay before it dawns.

1 John c. A.D. 100 All three letters of John are so like the Gospel of John* in style and doctrine* that it is highly likely they come from the same source. The first letter was written to the Christian communities in Asia, the existence of which was threatened by the onslaughts of the early heresies*. God is light – sin* turns light into darkness. We must keep the commandments*, especially that of love*; we must stand free of the world and be on the alert for the attacks of those who deny Christ's divinity. The Christian life is all summed up by faith* in Christ and love of the brethren.

2 John c. A.D. 100. A letter written to a Christian community in answer to those who were refusing to acknowledge that Christ, the Son of God, came in human nature.

3 John c. A.D. 100. A note to Gaius about the problem of Diotrephes who refuses to acknowledge the authority of the ministry* of the author and his companions.

Jude c. A.D. 90. The author denounces those who have infiltrated the faithful and are teaching falsehood. They will be punished for that, as well as for their irreligion and immorality. The faithful, however, must hold fast to and put their trust in God's love.

The Revelation of John possibly c. A.D. 95 or later. The book is totally different to any other document in the New Testament. It is an apocalyptic* document and has, therefore, some similarities with Daniel* in the Old Testament*. It was obviously written at a time when the Church* was suffering harsh persecution (possibly under Domitian) for being unwilling to sacrifice to the Emperor. The book's powerful visions were meant to strengthen the faithful and help them to hold on by promising better things to come. Names and places are disguised. The author embarks on warnings to seven churches after an initial vision. He then paints evocative pictures of God's throne in heaven, the Lamb (Jesus Christ), the breaking of the seven seals, the blowing of the seven trumpets, the woman and the dragon, the two beasts, the triumph of the Lamb, the seven bowls of plagues, the great prostitute, the fall of Babylon (i.e. Rome), the triumph of Christ, the thousand year reign and the new Jerusalem. The final victory is won. The Church's confidence in God's promises is unshaken. Hope abounds. The Lord will come.

13 Books

The Church's* life and worship* are broadly based on two books – the Bible* and a prayer book. The Bible is covered in detail in Section 12, but a list of Bibles available is included in this Section, together with lists of prayer books, and other books and services which have been authorised in the past, and are currently authorised for use, as well as a list of the most commonly used hymn books.

1 The Bible

The Authorised Version ('King James' Version'), 1611
The Revised Version, 1885
The Revised Standard Version, 1952
The Jerusalem Bible, 1966
The New English Bible, 1970
Today's English Version ('Good News Bible'), 1976
The New International Version, 1978
The New Jerusalem Bible, 1985
The Revised English Bible, 1989
The New Revised Standard Version 1989

2 Prayer Books

The First Prayer Book of Edward 6th (Cranmer – not in use), 1549
The Second Prayer Book of Edward 6th (Cranmer's further reforms – not in use), 1552
The Book of Common Prayer, 1662
The Deposited Book – the Book of Common Prayer, with alternative forms of service (rejected by Parliament), 1928
Revision Period – Series 1, Series 2, Series 1&2, Series 3 – 1966–1979.
The Alternative Service Book 1980 (not for use beyond December 2000)
The Common Worship series 2000

3 Psalters

The Psalter of the Book of Common Prayer (Coverdale – corrected version
    1540)
Revised Psalter (amended edition 1964)
The Psalter of the Standard Book of Common Prayer of the Episcopal Church
    in the U.S.A., considerably adjusted and inclusivized.

4 Other services and books

A Revised Catechism 1961
A Service for Remembrance Sunday, 1984

Although the following are not officially authorised, they are commended for
    use:
Services of Prayer and Dedication after Civil Marriage, 1985
Lent, Holy Week, Easter services and prayers (includes Night Prayer), 1987
The Promise of His Glory – services and prayers for the season from All Saints
    to Candlemas, 1991
Patterns for Worship, 1995

5 Hymn Books

The Church of England gives no specific direction on the use of hymn books;
    among the most widely used are:
Hymns Ancient and Modern – Revised or New Standard
Common Praise
New English Hymnal
Hymns for Today's Church
Mission Praise
Hymns Old and New

14. Signs and Symbols

Alpha and Omega The first and last letters of the Greek alphabet, used in the Christian Church* to denote God's infinity and eternity (Revelation* 1.8, 21.6) Their use is probably derived from the Hebrew word for 'truth', the first and last letters of which are the first and last letters of the Hebrew alphabet.

A.M.D.G. (Latin – *Ad Maiorem Dei Gloriam* – to the greater glory of God) Often used on memorials*, and to mark gifts to churches.

Chi Rho The first two letters of the Greek word for Christ: X = Ch, P = r.

Cross Keys A symbolic representation of the keys of the Kingdom of Heaven*, promised by our Lord to St Peter, and often used to signify the authority of a bishop* as a successor to the Apostles*.

D.O.M. (Latin – *Deo Optimo Maximo* – to God, the best and the greatest) Originally a pagan formula addressed to Jupiter, (especially that on the temple to Jupiter on the Capitol at Rome) it came to be widely used with a Christian application over the doors of churches and monuments*.

Dove The symbolic representation of the Holy Spirit* (Mark* 1.10)

Fish (Greek – *ichthus* – fish) A symbol of Christ or of the newly-baptised* or of the Eucharist*. It may be that the symbol is derived from the acrostic ΙΧΘΥΣ-Ιησοῦζ Χριστὸζ Θεοῦ ῾Χυιοζ Σωτήρ Jesus Christ of God Son Saviour.

I.H.S. (Greek – IHΣOYΣ – Jesus) The first three capital letters of the Greek word for Jesus. But once its use became established, it became corrupted to other Latin uses e.g. *Iesus Hominum Salvator* – Jesus, Saviour of mankind, or *In Hoc Signo* (vinces) – 'In this sign conquer' – deriving from the Emperor Constantine's vision which led to his conversion*.

I.N.R.I. The initial letters of the Latin words over the Cross of Christ, viz. *Iesus Nazarenus Rex Iudaeorum* – Jesus of Nazareth, the King of the Jews, frequently used as a sacred monogram.

Paschal Lamb The fulfilment of the Jewish Passover* in the Person of Christ has made him for Christians* the Paschal* Lamb. The use of a lamb as a symbol of Christ is based on such passages as John* 1.29, Revelation* 5.12. There are several types of this symbol, e.g. the lamb standing on Mount Sion (Revelation 14.1), the lamb carrying a crook and milk-pail (Revelation 7.17)

R.I.P. (Latin – *requiescat in pace* = may he/she rest in peace) A monogram often seen on tombs* and elsewhere expressing the hope of peace for the soul* of a dead person.

Ship A symbol of the Church* (see Dictionary section: **Ecumenism**, and Section 6: **Nave**)